PENGUIN BOOKS

AUTOCRACY, INC

A *Sunday Times, Telegraph, Financial Times, Economist* and *Observer* Book of the Year 2024

'A formidable authority on dictatorships . . . a clear-sighted and unflinching look at the ideas, resentments, assumptions and practices of the regimes that are challenging liberal democracy . . . offers an eloquent indictment of Western collusion in the creation of these autocracies'
Michael Ignatieff, Literary Review

'*Autocracy, Inc.* is clear-sighted and fearless . . . A masterful guide to the new age of autocracy lays bare the corruption and rot at the heart of authoritarian regimes . . . a masterclass in the marriage of dodgy government to international criminality . . . (both) deeply disturbing; it couldn't be anything else (and) a lively pleasure to read . . . It's a disturbing world we live in, but understanding its ways and knowing who to trust have never been so important. Anne Applebaum, who 30 years ago foresaw the way we were going, is one of those we can trust' John Simpson, *Guardian*

'Essential reading' Rachel Clarke, *Observer*, Books of the Year

'Applebaum deserves credit for drawing attention to the alarming new alliances of dictatorships seeking to shackle freedom, undermine human rights and usurp our values – along with the complacency of democracies that have done so little to stop the flood of fake news that infects our nations and dirty money that sustains our foes. "Nobody's democracy is safe,", Applebaum argues rightly' Ian Birrell, *Spectator*

'Vladimir Putin is not an isolated figure. As Applebaum shows, he is part of an informal network of autocrats that includes China, Iran, Venezuela and many others. In this elegantly written book, the American journalist argues that the new autocrats are often characterised by a desire to hold on to power and money rather than ideology'
Gideon Rachman, *Financial Times*, Books of the Year

'In her typically well-researched and readable *Autocracy, Inc*, Applebaum reminds us that there are considerably greater threats to our safety and security than political disagreement with domestic adversaries, not least the rise of such undemocratic states as Russia and China, who would collectively delight in the downfall of the West. If we aren't quite yet at that point, Applebaum shows us how it's far from unimaginable'
Alexander Larman, *Daily Telegraph*, Books of the Year

'A necessary, if anxiety-inducing read. Applebaum [is] long a scourge of repressive regimes . . . Having Applebaum's book in mind . . . is vividly to sense the underlying precariousness of our world. In many ways, Applebaum is the consummate witness of this new world order'
Tim Adams, *Observer*

'*Autocracy, Inc.* is a valuable book for many reasons, but the focus on illicit wealth creation and on those in democracies who enable it is especially timely. So is Applebaum's recommendation that we wage war on autocratic behaviors wherever they occur' Ruth Ben-Ghiat, *Washington Post*

'Anne Applebaum's *Autocracy, Inc.* provides a trenchant account that indicates that Trump, for all his bluster about America First, is part of a global phenomenon - namely, the rise of an international kleptocracy that often works in tandem' *Washington Monthly*

'Rigorously researched, bracing and realistic . . . But she is by no means fatalistic, urging free nations to confront the complicity of financial, legal and communications professionals in enabling *Autocracy, Inc*'
Matthew D'Ancona, *New European*

'The strength of *Autocracy, Inc.* lies in its description of how autocrats bend and distort opinion, and find allies across national boundaries'
Lloyd Green, *Guardian*

'*Autocracy, Inc.* charts the rise and rise of tyrannical leaders amid the end of history – and looks at Western complicity in their success . . . Applebaum is clear in exposing the thin threads separating the "free" and "tyrannical" worlds' Poppy Coburn, *Telegraph*

'Anne Applebaum is one of the wisest, best informed and most trenchant commentators on global politics. This book, which should be compulsory reading for every G7 head of government and foreign minister, sets out in disturbing detail the assault overt and covert by autocrats everywhere on liberal democracies and open societies. She demonstrates how we should not only fight for liberal values against Russia, China and all their cronies, but also live up to them ourselves'
Chris Patten, Former British Governor of Hong Kong

'A warning as to just how close we are to a subtler, more pervasive form of autocratic power, more fluid, easier to globalize . . . an important read'
LitHub

'Anne Applebaum's far-sighted book reveals an international network of autocrats who seek to subvert democracy in what has become a decentralized global struggle, with shifting alliances and no monolithic forces of good and evil. But it is also a practical manual packed with specific proposals to combat autocracy, in all its nefarious guises. Now it's up to us,the proponents of democracy – to step up and put these ideas into action' Garry Kasparov, Chess Grandmaster and author of *Winter Is Coming*

'Anne Applebaum is one of the most insightful observers of dictatorship, autocracy, tyranny, authoritarianism and democracy in the world today. *Autocracy, Inc.* is a wakeup call and offers a way ahead to anyone interested in preserving the democratic values and culture that have been fought for at a high price in blood and treasure for over 200 years' General Mark Milley, former Chairman of the Joint Chiefs of Staff

'Bold, powerful and important. Impunity is on the march because of the forces and tactics exposed here. We don't just need to read this book – we need to act on it' David Miliband, President and CEO of the International Rescue Committee and former Foreign Secretary of the United Kingdom

'A thoughtful and thought-provoking treatise on how autocracies have transformed from the way they operated in the 20th Century to the new modus operandi of the 21st . . . Applebaum is a skilled writer; her book is short, succinct, and compelling, and she is obviously passionate about and expert on the topic. An excellent read for anyone concerned about the fate of the liberal world order-in this country and, for that matter, universally' *Cipher Brief*

ABOUT THE AUTHOR

Anne Applebaum is the author of *Gulag: A History*, which won the Pulitzer Prize, of *Iron Curtain: The Crushing of Eastern Europe, 1944–1956*, which won the Cundill Prize, of *Red Famine: Stalin's War on Ukraine* which won the Lionel Gelber and Duff Cooper prizes, and of the best-selling *Twilight of Democracy*. She is a columnist for *The Atlantic* and a senior fellow at Johns Hopkins University. She divides her time between Britain, Poland and the USA.

AUTOCRACY, INC.

The Dictators Who Want to Run the World

Anne Applebaum

PENGUIN BOOKS

PENGUIN BOOKS

UK | USA | Canada | Ireland | Australia
India | New Zealand | South Africa

Penguin Books is part of the Penguin Random House group of companies
whose addresses can be found at global.penguinrandomhouse.com

Penguin Random House UK,
One Embassy Gardens, 8 Viaduct Gardens, London SW11 7BW

penguin.co.uk

Penguin Random House UK

First published in the United States of America by Doubleday,
a division of Penguin Random House LLC, New York 2024
First published in Great Britain by Allen Lane 2024
Published in Penguin Books with a new Preface 2025
001

Page 209 constitutes an extension of this copyright page

Printed and bound in Great Britain by Clays Ltd, Elcograf S.p.A.

The authorized representative in the EEA is Penguin Random House Ireland,
Morrison Chambers, 32 Nassau Street, Dublin D02 YH68

A CIP catalogue record for this book is available from the British Library

ISBN: 978-1-802-06212-0

Penguin Random House is committed to a sustainable future
for our business, our readers and our planet. This book is made from
Forest Stewardship Council® certified paper.

MIX
Paper | Supporting
responsible forestry
FSC® C018179
FSC
www.fsc.org

For the optimists

Contents

AUTOCRACY, INC.

Preface to the paperback edition

Autocracy, Inc. was first published in July 2024. In the months that followed, its central subject, the network of dictators who share common interests, not a common ideology, changed very little. Vladimir Putin, the Russian dictator, continued his illegal assault on the sovereign nation of Ukraine. Nicolas Maduro, the Venezuelan dictator, stayed in power even after Venezuelans voted overwhelmingly to remove him. The Syrian regime fell, but its prime allies, Iran and Russia, continued to try to influence its successors. Dictators from Azerbaijan to Zimbabwe, all members of the network I am calling Autocracy, Inc, continued to promote authoritarian narratives and opaque financial schemes, inside their own countries and around the world.

But during those same few months, the democratic world changed profoundly. In November 2024, the United States of America, for eighty years the leader of a powerful set of democratic alliances and an important promoter of democratic ideas around the world elected a president who was no longer interested in democracy, or democracies, at all. Instead, Donald Trump began to align American foreign and domestic policies with the values and practices of the autocratic world described in this book.

This dramatic shift was most visible in the new administration's relationships with America's historic allies. From his first days in office, President Trump attacked and berated Ukraine, Canada and the European Union, placing inexplicably high tariffs on goods coming from those countries, as well as from Japan and South Korea. He shouted at the Ukrainian president in the Oval Office, discussed the annexation of Greenland and Canada, and said that the EU had been created to "screw" the U.S. At the same time, he had few words of criticism for Russia, China, Iran or any of the other countries that have long colluded to undermine American political and economic power, as this book describes, and who have continued to do so during his presidency. His top aides agreed. "I fully share your loathing of European freeloading," American Secretary of Defense, Pete Hegseth texted other cabinet members in a leaked message: "It's PATHETIC."

This realignment away from the democratic world was accompanied by an equally revolutionary shift in official American attitudes to both domestic corruption and foreign kleptocracy. Perhaps no one should have been surprised: From the beginning of his career, well before he expressed much interest in politics, Donald Trump participated enthusiastically in the opaque, offshore world of shell companies and anonymous bank accounts, a milieu where the autocratic world thrives. From the 1980s onwards, anonymous investors were an important source of funding for Trump's real estate business. In that era, money from the former Soviet Union was pouring into opaque property investments, as Trump's son acknowledged in 2008: "In terms of high-end product influx into the US, Russians make up a pretty disproportionate cross-section of a lot of our assets." As of 2018, more than one out of every five condos in Trump-branded buildings was purchased by a shell company whose true owner is unknown. Anonymous owners continued to buy into his businesses even during his first term as president.

During that first term, Trump dodged or evaded conflict-of-interest rules designed to stop politicians from using political power to enrich themselves. During his second term he began to defy them with what can only be described as insouciance, immediately making clear that he and his family would both expand lucrative business relationships with the autocratic world and use their political influence for financial gain at home. In the weeks after the election, the Trump Organization announced construction of a Trump Tower in Saudi Arabia, an investment that created a clear conflict of interest for the president. Trump's family also created a crypto currency business, World Liberty Financial, that could, in practice, serve as a vehicle for anyone to pay him indirect bribes. Ominously, his administration did indeed suspend a civil investigation into Justin Sun, a Chinese entrepreneur and adviser to World Liberty Financial, who had also invested at least $75 million into the company.

In keeping with the new atmosphere, the inauguration itself became an ostentatious display of the new administration's kleptocratic values. American tech company CEOs were the most prominent guests, but several foreign business partners of the Trump Organization also attended inauguration-related events, posed for photos with Trump, and referenced their connections to his presidency in promotional materials. Several lesser-known companies involved in ongoing regulatory and other negotiations with the US government quietly donated hundreds of thousands to Trump's inauguration too. Soon afterwards, in a late-night purge, Trump fired seventeen inspectors-general, all people who are responsible for monitoring corruption and ethical violations inside the government.

Wealthy people have, it is true, always played an outsized role in American politics, as they do almost everywhere. But from the beginning of the second Trump term, one wealthy person was given a role that seems to have no precedent in American history. Elon Musk, who had no mandate other than the personal blessing of the president, was given enormous influence over the very same government institutions that had long subsidized and regulated his companies. Musk's so-called Department of Government Efficiency slashed jobs at the National Highway Traffic Safety Administration, the federal agency that oversees auto safety and crash investigations, including those involving his own company, Tesla. Musk oversaw mass firings at other regulatory agencies that had launched over 30 investigations into his companies, including SpaceX, Tesla, and Neuralink as well. Major government agencies, including the General Services Administration and the Federal Aviation Authority, began using or considering the use of Starlink, a product of SpaceX, while the State Department planned to buy armored Teslas.

Federal policy also made a sudden shift, in favor of opaque business practices and against ordinary Americans. The Treasury Department announced it would no longer penalize U.S. businesses and individuals that fail to disclose ownership information under the Corporate Transparency Act, hampering anti-money laundering efforts. Trump ordered a full work stoppage at the Consumer Financial Protection Bureau, which had been created to protect consumers from manipulation by banks and other financial institutions. He also fired top officials overseeing ethics, whistleblower protections, and labor rights, including the heads of the Office of Government Ethics, Office of Special Counsel, and the Merit Systems Protection Board.

A toxic combination of transactionalism and imperialism began to shape American foreign policy in ways that also have no precedent in contemporary history. During negotiations with President Volodymyr Zelensky of Ukraine, Trump's representatives handed Zelensky's team a memorandum of understanding, proposing that Ukraine hand over half of its mineral wealth, indefinitely. Trump's negotiations with Russia, meanwhile, were from the start dominated not by a desire to create a just and lasting peace in Ukraine, but by a desire to help American businesses, and perhaps his family's businesses, profit from the lifting of Russian sanctions. Trump's erratic tariffs, meanwhile, offered him the opportunity to negotiate individual deals with other countries, as well as with American and foreign businesses, giving him unprecedented power.

Trump's domestic policies reflected the same reorientation: Away from the rule of law, away from institutions created by Congress, and towards the personalization of power. Under the false flag of cost-saving, Musk's DOGE carried out mass firings and program cuts, making no attempt to audit or even understand many of the institutions affected. Among them were America's foreign broadcasters, including Voice of America, Radio Free Europe/Radio Liberty, Radio Free Asia and other media which have for decades practiced independent journalism in parts of the world that don't have it. Musk slashed funding for organizations who campaign for democracy and voting rights. He destroyed USAID, the aid organization whose humanitarian programs provided food and medicine to the poorest people on the planet. All of these programs had long provided a counterweight to the Russian, Chinese, Iranian and other influence campaigns which the Trump administration, clearly, was no longer interested in fighting.

Musk claimed he cut these programs because he wanted to save money. But that explanation, given that they represent a tiny fraction of the U.S. budget, was insufficient. Instead, their destruction, alongside the damage done to domestic departments and agencies overseeing education, scientific research, health and social security, seemed deliberately designed to alter the behavior and values of the civil service. Since the late nineteenth century, federal workers in America had been trained to respect the rule of law, venerate the Constitution, maintain political neutrality, and uphold lawful policy changes whether they come from Republican or Democratic administrations. They were supposed to measure objective reality—evidence of pollution, for example—and respond accordingly. The non-partisan values of this system had long been accepted by everyone, from Republican-voting FBI agents to Democratic-voting environmental officers.

During their early weeks in office, Trump's cabinet began plotting to replace these civil servants with loyalists chosen not by merit tests, but by purity tests. Already in the first weeks of the administration, at least two candidates for higher positions at the FBI were told to state who the "real patriots" were on January 6, 2021. They were asked, in other words, not just to demonstrate their fealty to Trump, but also to repeat outright falsehoods, violating the old civil-service ethos which required people to make decisions based on objective realities, not myths or fictions.

The impact of this change was rapid, and harsh. Suddenly, and not accidentally, people who worked for the American federal government had the same experience as people who find themselves living under foreign occupation. In March of 2025, I received a letter from a woman who had worked for much of her career at major universities and as a government scientist. She had read an article I had written about the experience of living through regime change, and found it touched a chord. She too, she said, "will soon face a choice about whether to allow myself to get fired, to resign, or to be considered complicit in the current regime." These are not choices that Americans are used to making. But they would sound very familiar to the inhabitants of the autocratic world described in this book.

So too would Trump's use of lawsuits to intimidate the media. Or his attempts to browbeat Republican congressmen and Senators, using financial threats to their future campaigns. Or his administration's selective targeting of foreign students, some of whom were picked up on the street by plain clothes officers. Or his threats to law firms who defend clients he doesn't like. Or the deportation without due process of immigrants, including immigrants with legal status, to prisons in El Salvador.

Put all these changes together, and there is a pattern. A personalized, even patrimonial foreign policy, one designed not to benefit America's allies, or even America itself, but rather to benefit the American president, his friends and his family. A political system designed to reward people for loyalty, not for merit. A drumbeat of propaganda directed against judges, journalists, whistleblowers, anyone who stands in the way of the regime. These are the features of the states that comprise Autocracy, Inc., and they now describe the political system that the Trump administration is trying to build in the United States.

Americans who believe in the rule of law, European and Asian allies who have long argued in favor of American leadership, democratic activists around the world who admired what America stood for – all of them, all of us, need to rethink how we approach the world in light of these dramatic changes. Yet the advice I give at the end of this book still holds. Broad, powerful, carefully focused coalitions are still the only way that the democratic world can resist the influence of autocratic propaganda, and autocratic corruption. Now we will simply have to form them, at least temporarily, without the leadership of the United States.

Anne Applebaum
April 2025

Introduction

Autocracy, Inc.

All of us have in our minds a cartoon image of an autocratic state. There is a bad man at the top. He controls the army and the police. The army and the police threaten the people with violence. There are evil collaborators, and maybe some brave dissidents.

But in the twenty-first century, that cartoon bears little resemblance to reality. Nowadays, autocracies are run not by one bad guy but by sophisticated networks relying on kleptocratic financial structures, a complex of security services—military, paramilitary, police—and technological experts who provide surveillance, propaganda, and disinformation. The members of these networks are connected not only to one another within a given autocracy but also to networks in other autocratic countries, and sometimes in democracies too. Corrupt, state-controlled companies in one dictatorship do business with corrupt, state-controlled companies in another. The police in one country may arm, equip, and train the police in many others. The propagandists share resources—the troll farms and media networks that promote one dictator's propaganda can also be used to promote another's—as well as themes: the degeneracy of democracy, the stability of autocracy, the evil of America.

This is not to say that there is some secret room where bad guys meet, as in a James Bond movie. Nor is our conflict with them a black-and-white, binary contest, a "Cold War 2.0." Among modern autocrats are people who call themselves communists, monarchists, nationalists, and theocrats. Their regimes have different historical roots, different goals, different aesthetics. Chinese communism and Russian nationalism differ not only from each other but from Venezuela's Bolivarian socialism, North Korea's *Juche,* or the Shia radicalism of the Islamic Republic of Iran. All of them differ from the Arab monarchies and others—Saudi Arabia, the Emirates, Vietnam—which mostly don't seek to undermine the democratic world. They also differ from the softer autocracies and hybrid democracies, sometimes called illiberal democracies—Turkey, Singapore, India, the Philippines, Hungary—which sometimes align with the democratic world and sometimes don't. Unlike military or political alliances from other times and places, this group operates not like a bloc but rather like an agglomeration of companies, bound not by ideology but rather by a ruthless, single-minded determination to preserve their personal wealth and power: Autocracy, Inc.

Instead of ideas, the strongmen who lead Russia, China, Iran, North Korea, Venezuela, Nicaragua, Angola, Myanmar, Cuba, Syria, Zimbabwe, Mali, Belarus, Sudan, Azerbaijan, and perhaps three dozen others share a determination to deprive their citizens of any real influence or public voice, to push back against all forms of transparency or accountability, and to repress anyone, at home or abroad, who challenges them. They also share a brutally pragmatic approach to wealth. Unlike the fascist and communist leaders of the past, who had party machines behind them and did not showcase their greed, the leaders of Autocracy, Inc., often maintain opulent residences and structure much of their collaboration as for-profit ventures. Their bonds with one another, and with their friends in the democratic world, are cemented not through ideals but through deals—deals designed to take the edge off sanctions, to exchange surveillance technology, to help one another get rich.

Autocracy, Inc., also collaborates to keep its members in power. Alexander Lukashenko's unpopular regime in Belarus has been criticized by multiple international bodies—the European Union, the Organization for Security and Cooperation in Europe—and shunned by its European neighbors. Many Belarusian goods cannot be sold in the United States or the EU. The national airline, Belavia, cannot fly to European countries. And yet, in practice, Belarus is not isolated at all. More than two dozen Chinese companies have invested money in Belarus, even building a China-Belarus Industrial Park, modeled on a similar project in Suzhou. Iran and Belarus exchanged high-level diplomatic visits in 2023. Cuban officials have expressed solidarity with Lukashenko at the UN. Russia offers markets, cross-border investment, political support, and probably police and security services too. In 2020, when Belarusian journalists rebelled and refused to report a false election result, Russia sent Russian journalists to replace them. In return, Belarus's regime has allowed Russia to base troops and weapons on its territory and to use those assets to attack Ukraine.

Venezuela is also, in theory, an international pariah. Since 2008, the United States, Canada, and the European Union have ramped up sanctions on Venezuela in response to the regime's brutality, drug smuggling, and links to international crime. Yet President Nicolás Maduro's regime receives loans from Russia, which also invests in Venezuela's oil industry, as does Iran. A Belarusian company assembles tractors in Venezuela. Turkey facilitates the illicit Venezuelan gold trade. Cuba has long provided security advisers and security technology to its counterparts in Caracas. Chinese-made water cannons, tear-gas canisters, and shields were used to crush street protesters in Caracas in 2014 and again in 2017, leaving more than seventy dead, while Chinese-designed surveillance technology is used to monitor the public too. Meanwhile, the international narcotics trade keeps individual members of the regime, along with their entourages and families, well supplied with Versace and Chanel.

The Belarusian and Venezuelan dictators are widely despised within their own countries. Both would lose free elections, if such elections were ever held. Both have powerful opponents: the Belarusian and the Venezuelan opposition movements have been led by a range of charismatic leaders and dedicated grassroots activists who have inspired their fellow citizens to take risks, to work for change, to come out onto the streets in protest. In August 2020, more than a million Belarusians, out of a population of only ten million, protested in the streets against stolen elections. Hundreds of thousands of Venezuelans repeatedly participated in protests across the country too.

If their only enemies had been the corrupt, bankrupt Venezuelan regime or the brutal, ugly Belarusian regime, these protest movements might have won. But they were not fighting autocrats only at home; they were fighting autocrats around the world who control state companies in multiple countries and who can use them to make investment decisions worth billions of dollars. They were fighting regimes that can buy security cameras from China or bots from St. Petersburg. Above all, they were fighting against rulers who long ago hardened themselves to the feelings and opinions of their countrymen, as well as the feelings and opinions of everybody else. Autocracy, Inc., offers its members not only money and security but also something less tangible: impunity.

The conviction, common among the most committed autocrats, that the outside world cannot touch them—that the views of other nations don't matter and that no court of public opinion will ever judge them—is relatively recent. Once upon a time the leaders of the Soviet Union, the most powerful autocracy in the second half of the twentieth century, cared deeply about how they were perceived around the world. They vigorously promoted the superiority of their political system, and they objected when it was criticized. They at least paid lip service to the aspirational system of norms and treaties set up after World War II, with its language about universal human rights, the laws of war, and the rule of law more generally. When the Soviet premier Nikita Khrushchev stood up in the United Nations and banged his shoe on the table, as he famously did in the General Assembly in 1960, it was because a Filipino delegate said that Soviet-occupied Eastern Europe had been "deprived of political and civil rights" and "swallowed up by the Soviet Union." Khrushchev felt it was important to object. Even in the early part of this century, most dictatorships hid their true intentions behind elaborate, carefully manipulated performances of democracy.

Today, the members of Autocracy, Inc., no longer care if they or their countries are criticized or by whom. Some, like the leaders of Myanmar and Zimbabwe, don't stand for anything beyond self-enrichment and the desire to remain in power, and so can't be embarrassed. The leaders of Iran confidently discount the views of Western infidels. The leaders of Cuba and Venezuela treat criticism from abroad as evidence of the vast imperial plot organized against them. The leaders of China and Russia have spent a decade disputing the human rights language long used by international institutions, successfully convincing many around the world that the treaties and conventions on war and genocide—and concepts such as "civil liberties" and "the rule of law"—embody Western ideas that don't apply to them.

Impervious to international criticism, modern autocrats feel no shame about the use of open brutality. The Burmese junta does not hide the fact that it has murdered hundreds of protesters, including young teenagers, on the streets of

Rangoon. The Zimbabwean regime harasses opposition candidates in plain sight during farcical fake elections. The Chinese government boasts about its destruction of the popular democracy movement in Hong Kong and its "anti-extremist" campaign—involving mass arrests and concentration camps for thousands of Muslim Uighurs—in Xinjiang. The Iranian regime does not conceal its violent repression of Iranian women.

At the extremes, such contempt can devolve into what the international democracy activist Srdja Popovic has called the "Maduro model" of governance, after the current leader of Venezuela. Autocrats who adopt it are "willing to see their country enter the category of failed states," he says—accepting economic collapse, endemic violence, mass poverty, and international isolation if that's what it takes to stay in power. Like Maduro, Presidents Bashir al-Assad in Syria and Lukashenko in Belarus seem entirely comfortable ruling over collapsed economies and societies. These kinds of regimes can be hard for the inhabitants of democracies to understand, because their primary goal is not to create prosperity or enhance the well-being of citizens. Their primary goal is to stay in power, and to do so, they are willing to destabilize their neighbors, destroy the lives of ordinary people, or—following in the footsteps of their predecessors—even send hundreds of thousands of their citizens to their deaths.

In the twentieth century, the autocratic world was no more unified than it is today. Communists and fascists went to war with each other. Sometimes communists fought communists too. But they did have common views about the political system that Lenin, the founder of the Soviet state, referred to sneeringly as "bourgeois democracy," which he called "restricted, truncated, false, and hypocritical, a paradise for the rich and a snare and deception for the exploited, for the poor." "Pure democracy" he wrote, was "the mendacious phrase of a liberal who wants to fool the workers." As the leader of what was originally a tiny political faction, Lenin was, unsurprisingly, dismissive of the idea of free elections too: "Only scoundrels and simpletons can think that the proletariat must first win a majority in elections carried out under the yoke of the bourgeoisie. . . . This is the height of stupidity."

The founders of fascism, although bitterly opposed to Lenin's regime, were equally dismissive about their democratic opponents. Mussolini, the Italian leader whose movement coined the words "fascism" and "totalitarianism," mocked liberal societies as weak and degenerate. "The liberal state is destined to perish," he predicted in 1932. "All the political experiments of our day are anti-liberal." He also flipped the definition of "democracy," defining the Italian and German dictatorships as "the greatest and soundest democracies which exist in the world today." Hitler's critique of liberalism followed the same pattern. He wrote in *Mein Kampf* that parliamentary democracy is "one of the most serious signs of decay in mankind" and declared that it is not "individual freedom which is a sign of a higher level of culture but the restriction of individual freedom," if carried out by a racially pure organization.

As early as 1929, Mao Zedong, who later became the dictator of the People's Republic of China, also warned against what he called "ultra-democracy," because "these ideas are utterly incompatible with the fighting tasks of the proletariat"—a statement later reproduced in his *Little Red Book*. One of the founding documents of the modern Myanmar regime, a 1962 memo titled "The Burmese Way to Socialism," contains a tirade against elected legislatures: "Burma's 'parliamentary democracy' has not only failed to serve our socialist development but also, due to its very inconsistencies, defects, weaknesses and loopholes, its abuses and the absence of a mature public opinion, lost sight of and deviated from the socialist aims."

Sayyid Qutb, one of the intellectual founders of modern radical Islam, borrowed both the communist belief in a universal revolution and the fascist belief in the liberating power of violence. Like Hitler and Stalin, he argued that liberal ideas and modern commerce posed a threat to the creation of an ideal civilization—in this case, Islamic civilization. He built an ideology around opposition to democracy and individual rights, crafting a cult of destruction and death. The Iranian scholars and human rights activists Ladan and Roya Boroumand have written that Qutb imagined that an "ideologically self-conscious, vanguard minority" would lead a violent revolution in order to create an ideal society, "a classless one where the 'selfish individual' of liberal democracies would be banished and the 'exploitation of man by man' would be abolished. God alone would govern it through the implementation of Islamic law (*shari'a*)." This, they write, was "Leninism in Islamist dress."

Modern autocrats differ in many ways from their twentieth-century predecessors. But the heirs, successors, and imitators of these older leaders and thinkers, however varied their ideologies, do have a common enemy. That enemy is us.

To be more precise, that enemy is the democratic world, "the West," NATO, the European Union, their own, internal democratic opponents, and the liberal ideas that inspire all of them. These include the notion that the law is a neutral force, not subject to the whims of politics; that courts and judges should be independent; that political opposition is legitimate; that the rights to speech and assembly can be guaranteed; and that there can be independent journalists and writers and thinkers who are capable of being critical of the ruling party or leader while at the same time remaining loyal to the state.

Autocrats hate these principles because they threaten their power. If judges and juries are independent, then they can hold rulers to account. If there is a genuinely free press, journalists can expose high-level theft and corruption. If the political system empowers citizens to influence the government, then citizens can eventually change the regime.

Their enmity toward the democratic world is not merely some form of traditional geopolitical competition, as "realists" and so many international relations strategists still believe. Their opposition rather has its roots in the very nature of the democratic political system, in words like "accountability," "transparency," and "democracy." They hear that language coming from the democratic world, they hear the same language coming from their own dissidents, and they seek to destroy them both. Their own rhetoric makes this clear. In 2013, as Xi Jinping was beginning his rise to power, an internal Chinese memo known, enigmatically, as Document Number Nine or, more formally, as the "Communiqué on the Current State of the Ideological Sphere," listed the "seven perils" faced by the Chinese Communist Party (CCP). Western constitutional democracy led the list, followed by "universal values," media independence and civic participation, as well as "nihilist" criticism of the Communist Party. The now-infamous document concluded that "Western forces hostile to China," together with dissidents inside the country, "are still constantly infiltrating the ideological sphere." The document went on to instruct party leaders to push back against these ideas and to control them in public spaces, above all on the internet, wherever they found them.

Since at least 2004, the Russians have focused on the same set of threats. In that year, Ukrainians staged a popular revolt, known as the Orange Revolution—the name came from the orange T-shirts and orange flags of the protesters—against a clumsy attempt to steal a presidential election. The angry intervention of the Ukrainian public into what was meant to have been a carefully manipulated, orchestrated victory for Viktor Yanukovych, a pro-Russian candidate directly supported by Putin himself, profoundly unnerved the Russians, especially since a similarly unruly protest movement in Georgia had brought a pro-European politician, Mikheil Saakashvili, to power the year before. Shaken by those two events, Putin put the bogeyman of "color revolution" at the center of Russian propaganda. Civic protest movements are always described as "color revolutions" in Russia and as the work of outsiders. Popular leaders are always said to be foreign puppets. Anticorruption and pro-democracy slogans are linked to chaos and instability. In 2011, a year of mass protest against a manipulated election in Russia itself, Putin evoked the Orange Revolution with real bitterness, describing it as a "well-tested scheme for destabilizing society" and accusing the Russian opposition of "transferring this practice to Russian soil," where he feared a similar popular uprising intended to remove him from power.

He was wrong; there was no "scheme" that was "transferred." Public discontent in Russia, like public discontent in China, simply had nowhere to express itself except through street protest. Putin's opponents had no legal means to remove him from power. Critics of the regime talk about democracy and human rights in Russia because it reflects their experience of injustice, and not only in Russia. The protests that led to democratic transitions in the Philippines, Taiwan, South Africa, South Korea, Myanmar, and Mexico; the "people's revolutions" that washed across central and Eastern Europe in 1989; the Arab Spring in 2011; and the Hong Kong protests of 2019–20 were all begun by people who had experienced injustice at the hands of the state.

This is the core of the problem: the leaders of Autocracy, Inc., know that the language of transparency, accountability, justice, and democracy will always appeal to some of their own citizens. To stay in power they must undermine those ideas, wherever they are found.

On February 24, 2022, Russia launched a full-scale war against Ukraine, the first full-scale kinetic battle in the struggle between Autocracy, Inc., and what might loosely be described as the democratic world. Russia plays a special role in the autocratic network, both as the inventor of the modern marriage of kleptocracy and dictatorship and as the country now most aggressively seeking to upend the status quo. The invasion was planned in that spirit. Putin hoped not only to acquire territory, but also to show the world that the old rules of international behavior no longer hold.

From the very first days of the war, Putin and the Russian security elite ostentatiously demonstrated their disdain for the language of human rights, their disregard for the laws of war, their scorn for international law and for treaties they themselves had signed. They arrested public officials and civic leaders: mayors, police officers, civil servants, school directors, journalists, artists, museum curators. They built torture chambers for civilians in most of the towns they occupied in southern and eastern Ukraine. They kidnapped thousands of children, ripping some away from their families, removing others from orphanages, gave them new "Russian" identities, and prevented them from returning home to Ukraine. They deliberately targeted emergency workers. Brushing aside the principles of territorial integrity that Russia had accepted in the United Nations Charter and the Helsinki Accords, Putin announced, in the summer of 2022, that he would annex territory that his army did not even control. Occupying forces stole and exported Ukrainian grain and "nationalized" Ukrainian factories and mines, handing them over to Russian businessmen close to Putin, making a mockery of international property law as well.

These acts were not collateral damage or accidental side effects of the war. They were part of a conscious plan to undermine the network of ideas, rules, and treaties that had been built into international law since 1945, to destroy the European order created after 1989, and, most important, to damage the influence and reputation of the United States and its democratic allies. "This is not about Ukraine at all, but the world order," said Sergei Lavrov, the Russian foreign minister, soon after the war began. "The current crisis is a fateful, epoch-making moment in modern history. It reflects the battle over what the world order will look like."

Putin thought that he would get away with these crimes and win quickly, both because he knew very little about modern Ukraine, which he believed would not defend itself, and because he expected the democracies to bow to his wishes. He assumed that the deep political divisions in the United States and Europe, some of which he had actively encouraged, would incapacitate the leaders. He reckoned that the European business community, some of which he had long courted, would demand a resumption of Russian trade.

Decisions taken in Washington, London, Paris, Brussels, Berlin, and Warsaw—not to mention Tokyo, Seoul,

Ottawa, and Canberra—in the wake of the 2022 invasion initially proved Putin wrong. The democratic world quickly imposed harsh sanctions on Russia, froze Russian state assets, and removed Russian banks from international payment systems. A consortium of more than fifty countries provided arms, intelligence, and money to the Ukrainian government. Sweden and Finland, both countries that had maintained political neutrality for decades, decided to join NATO. Olaf Scholz, the German chancellor, declared his country had come to a *Zeitenwende,* a "turning point," and agreed to contribute German weapons to a European war for the first time since 1945. The American president, Joe Biden, described the moment during a speech in Warsaw as a test for America, for Europe, and for the transatlantic alliance.

"Would we stand up for the sovereignty of nations?" Biden asked. "Would we stand up for the right of people to live free from naked aggression? Would we stand up for democracy?"

Yes, he concluded, to loud applause: "We would be strong. We would be united."

But if Putin had underestimated the unity of the democratic world, the democracies also underestimated the scale of the challenge. Like the democracy activists of Venezuela or Belarus, they slowly learned that they were not merely fighting Russia in Ukraine. They were fighting Autocracy, Inc.

Xi Jinping had signaled his support for Russia's illegal invasion before it began, issuing a joint statement with the Russian president on February 4, less than three weeks before the first bombs fell on Kyiv. Anticipating American and European outrage, the two leaders declared in advance their intention to ignore any criticism of Russian actions, and especially anything that resembled "interference in the internal affairs of sovereign states under the pretext of protecting democracy and human rights." Although Xi never shared the Russian leader's obsession with the destruction of Ukraine, and although the Chinese seemed eager to avoid nuclear escalation, they refused to criticize Russia directly as the war dragged on. Instead, they profited from the new situation, bought Russian oil and gas at low prices, and quietly sold defense technology to Russia too.

They were not alone. As the war progressed, Iran exported thousands of lethal drones to Russia. North Korea supplied ammunition and missiles. Russian client states and friends in Africa, including Eritrea, Zimbabwe, Mali, and the Central African Republic, backed Russia at the UN and elsewhere. From the very early days of the war, Belarus allowed Russian troops to use its territory, including roads, railway lines, and military bases. Turkey, Georgia, Kyrgyzstan, and Kazakhstan, all illiberal states with transactional ties to the autocratic world, helped the Russian defense industry evade sanctions and import machine tools and electronics. India took advantage of lowered prices and bought Russian oil.

By the spring of 2023, Russian officials had become more ambitious. They began to discuss the creation of a Eurasian digital currency, perhaps based on blockchain technology, to replace the dollar and diminish American economic influence around the world. They also planned to deepen their relationship with China, to share research into artificial intelligence and the Internet of Things. The ultimate purpose of all this activity was never in doubt. A leaked document describing these discussions summed them up by echoing Lavrov's words: Russia should aim "to create a new world order."

That goal is widely shared. Shored up by the technologies and tactics they copy from one another, by their common economic interests, and above all by their determination not to give up power, the autocracies believe that they are winning. That belief—where it came from, why it persists, how the democratic world originally helped consolidate it, and how we can now defeat it—is the subject of this book.

1

The Greed That Binds

IN THE SUMMER of 1967, Austrian and West German capitalists from the gas and steel industries met a group of Soviet communists in the quiet confines of an old Habsburg hunting lodge near Vienna. The atmosphere must have been strange. Soviet troops had left Austria only twelve years earlier. West German soldiers still stared down East German soldiers across a fortified border between their respective countries. Fears of imminent Soviet invasion had faded, but only thanks to the large American military presence in Europe.

Nevertheless, everyone in the room had interests in common. Soviet engineers had just discovered huge gas fields in western Siberia. New technology meant that gas was becoming cleaner, cheaper, and easier to transport. Pipelines from the communist East to the capitalist West seemed an excellent way for both sides to benefit. The group talked and agreed to meet again. The conversation then continued in other cities, moving from the price of gas to the cost of loans to the technology of pipeline construction. In February 1970, West German and Soviet officials finally concluded the agreement that would lead to the construction of the first gas pipelines from the U.S.S.R. to Western Europe.

Prior to that deal, economic exchange between Western Europe or the United States and the Soviet Union had been minimal, involving nothing much more complex than trade in icons, timber, and grain, plus a few dodgy mining deals. From the moment the hunting lodge talks began in Austria, everyone knew that the gas trade would be different. Pipelines were expensive and permanent. They could not be laid down one day, removed the next, and they could not depend upon the whim of a particular leader. There had to be long-term contracts, and these contracts had to be enveloped within a set of predictable political relationships.

For Willy Brandt, the West German foreign minister at the time, these predictable relationships were a large part of the project's appeal. He did not fear that his country would become dependent on the Soviet Union. On the contrary, he leaned on his negotiators, urging them to make the deal bigger. His reasoning was mostly political: he believed that a mutually dependent economic relationship would make a future military conflict unthinkable. As chancellor, which he eventually became, Brandt made his *Ostpolitik*—his "eastern policy"—one of the central pillars of postwar German foreign policy. In subsequent years, the pipelines provided a physical link between Moscow and Bonn, and eventually Berlin, Rome, Amsterdam, Helsinki, and dozens of other European cities. They remained at the center of German foreign policy after 1991, when the Soviet Union broke up and Germany reunited.

Along the way, Germany's *Ostpolitik* also became a theory of change, explaining not merely how democracies could trade with autocracies but how they could slowly and subtly alter them. Egon Bahr, a longtime adviser to Brandt, described the idea in a famous speech in 1963, calling this concept *Wandel durch Annäherung* (change through rapprochement). If the West could tone down the confrontation, engage with the East German regime, and offer trade instead of boycotts, he argued, then a "loosening of the borders" might be possible. Bahr never called for boycotts or sanctions against the East Germans and rarely mentioned political prisoners, even though he knew the political prisoners were there: West Germany frequently paid for the release of dissidents from East German prisons, spending more than 3 billion deutsche marks on this strange human trade in the years before 1989. Instead of speaking clearly about prisoners or human rights, Bahr deployed what the writer Timothy Garton Ash has called "emotive imprecision" to evade the subject.

Not everyone else was so certain about the pipeline deals. Richard Nixon always believed that the Soviet Union's true purpose in trading and talking with Brandt and Bahr was, as Nixon put it, "to detach Germany from NATO." Jimmy Carter, who wanted to prioritize the promotion of human rights over trade, disliked *Ostpolitik* so much that he imposed a boycott on the sale of some U.S. pipeline technology to Germany after the Soviet Union imprisoned two dissidents,

Aleksandr Ginzburg and Natan Sharansky, in 1978. Helmut Schmidt, German chancellor at the time, fumed that Carter was an "idealistic preacher" who knew nothing about Russia. The Reagan administration took a step further, placing export controls on some pipeline equipment following the declaration of martial law in Poland in 1981, blocking American companies from working on the pipeline, and banning foreign companies involved in the project from doing business in the United States, all radical moves at the time.

Nixon, Carter, and Reagan were motivated by neither spite nor pure commercial self-interest, but rather by questions about the political consequences of trade with an autocracy. Although Germany was the prime contractor, the gas benefited many countries, potentially making the entire continent dependent on Soviet goodwill. Could the pipelines be used as blackmail? Reagan's defense secretary, Caspar Weinberger, worried out loud about the need to limit "Soviet economic leverage over the West."

Underlying this conversation lay a deeper moral and political question: Did East–West trade enrich and empower the Soviet state and its empire? From the time of the Bolshevik Revolution, the Kremlin's foreign policy goals had explicitly included the subversion of European democracies. During the 1970s and 1980s, the U.S.S.R. supported terrorist groups in West Germany and Italy, aided extremist movements across the Continent and around the world, and suppressed political opposition in Eastern Europe, including East Germany. Nevertheless, gas kept flowing west and hard currency flowed east, providing Moscow with funding that helped sustain the same Red Army that NATO had to be prepared to fight and the same KGB that Western security services competed against. If this trade empowered Moscow, was it really beneficial? What were the hidden costs? While the Soviet Union existed, this paradox of U.S. and European policy was never really resolved, and it remained unresolved after the U.S.S.R. broke apart.

In the 1990s, an era when most people expected to enjoy the new peace dividend and spend the rest of the time talking about television shows, the hidden costs of anything were hardly mentioned at all. This was the era of Francis Fukuyama's "End of History?," the 1989 *National Interest* essay that was widely misread as a statement of naive, everything-is-for-the-best-in-the-best-of-all-possible-worlds good cheer. *Liberal democracy is victorious, sooner or later everyone will want it, and no special effort is required to promote it; just be patient, and the beneficial effects of trade and globalization will work their magic.* Fukuyama's actual argument was more subtle than that, but the simplified version became popular because people wanted it to be true.

And no wonder: The idea that there was something preordained, even inevitable, about liberal democracy had a deep appeal. It made the inhabitants of democracies feel virtuous, since they already lived in the ideal society. It made the businessmen and bankers who were just then beginning to expand their investments into China and the post-Soviet world feel better too. If the old moral dilemmas about investing in autocracy were gone, then there was nothing special they needed to do to justify their actions.

It was around this time that Bahr's old phrase *Wandel durch Annäherung,* "change through rapprochement," morphed into *Wandel durch Handel*—"change through trade." This pleasing rhyme not only sounded better in German; it also reflected reality. Trade among the postwar democracies in Western Europe, in the form of the increasingly integrated common market, really had produced peace and prosperity. After 1990, many hoped trade would also enrich the eastern half of the Continent and bring it closer, politically and culturally, to the western half. *Wandel durch Handel* became popular partly because it suited the world of commerce but also because it described the actual experience of ordinary people.

So much confidence was placed in the efficacy of trade that some quickly forgot the harder-edged policies that also contributed to European reunification. In 2014, Berlin marked the twenty-fifth anniversary of the fall of the Berlin Wall, and I attended the formal celebrations, led by the German chancellor, Angela Merkel. Mikhail Gorbachev was in the room, as a kind of victory token, as was Lech Wałęsa. But President George H. W. Bush, who had actually negotiated the end of the Soviet Union and the breakup of the Soviet Empire, was scarcely mentioned. Nor did the American troops who helped deter Soviet attack for so many decades, and who were (and still are) based in Germany, get much attention. Violence, soldiers, armies, and above all nuclear weapons had been written out of the story.

The Germans believed that trade and diplomacy had reunited their country. They also believed that trade and diplomacy would, eventually, help normalize relations between Russia and Europe. At the same time, and for similar reasons, many Americans and Europeans came to believe that trade would also bring harmony to the Pacific, by integrating China into the democratic world. They too had grounds for hope: different factions were jockeying for power in China, including some that wanted liberal reforms. As the scholar Julian Gewirtz has recently written, Chinese economists in this era maintained a surprisingly wide array of contacts with Western economists, borrowing their analysis of markets and trade as well as their understanding of the links between economic growth and political culture. A more liberal China, if not exactly a democratic China, seemed well within reach, including to many Chinese.

Nevertheless, it is remarkable, in retrospect, how quickly so many Western analysts and leaders from across the political spectrum leaped upon the most optimistic of all possible scenarios. As early as 1984, just a few years into Deng Xiaoping's reforms, Ronald Reagan visited China and declared, in a sunny, optimistic, upbeat speech, that "there's much to be gained on both sides from expanded opportunities in trade and commerce and cultural relations." He was sure he had seen signs of a deeper change: "The first injection of free market spirit has already enlivened the Chinese economy. I believe it has also made a contribution to human happiness in China and opened the way to a more just society."

More than a decade later, Bill Clinton, a president of a

different generation and a different political persuasion, declared that "growing interdependence would have a liberalizing effect in China. . . . Computers and the Internet, fax machines and photo-copiers, modems and satellites all increase the exposure to people, ideas, and the world beyond China's borders." In 2000, when arguing for China to be admitted to the World Trade Organization, he stated this case even more emphatically. "I believe the choice between economic rights and human rights, between economic security and national security, is a false one," he told an audience at the Johns Hopkins School of Advanced International Studies. The transcript records the audience reactions:

> Now there's no question China has been trying to crack down on the Internet. (*Chuckles.*)
>
> Good luck! (*Laughter.*)
>
> That's sort of like trying to nail jello to the wall. (*Laughter.*)

Clinton's optimism, in retrospect, was extraordinary. "In the knowledge economy," he said, "economic innovation and political empowerment, whether anyone likes it or not, will inevitably go hand in hand." The optimism was also widely shared. In 2008, Gerhard Schröder, the German chancellor who was a rough contemporary of Clinton's, wrote an article titled "Why We Need Beijing," lauding what he said were the signs of "progress on China's path to a constitutional, just, and one day, I am sure, also democratic society" and calling on Germany to "have a trusting and fair dialogue with the country so that standards of the rule of law, freedom, and, at the end of a development path, democracy prevail."

There were skeptics as well. A broad coalition of politicians and trade unionists tried to stop Chinese entry into the World Trade Organization, fearing the effects on Western workers. Others simply doubted whether the relationship could deliver what it promised. Chris Patten, the last British governor of Hong Kong, has said that Britain was "delusional" for imagining that a wealthier China would automatically become a democracy. But amid all the discussion about China and Russia that took place in the 1990s, and despite all the debate about the *economic* impact that open borders might have on Western markets, almost no one spoke about the *political* impact on Western democracies.

Everyone assumed that in a more open, interconnected world, democracy and liberal ideas would spread to the autocratic states. Nobody imagined that autocracy and illiberalism would spread to the democratic world instead.

Autocracy is a political system, a way of structuring society, a means of organizing power. It is not a genetic trait. Particular cultures, languages, or religions do not necessarily produce it. No nation is condemned forever to autocracy, just as no nation is guaranteed democracy. Political systems do change. In the late 1980s, during the explosion of public conversation and debate known as glasnost, many Russians believed that Russia could change.

More than that, many Russians in this era believed their

country was on the verge of a historic, positive transformation, perhaps even a liberal democratic transformation. *Izvestiya,* the house newspaper of the Soviet government, declared that "the crushed and eviscerated ideas of democracy and liberty begin to gather momentum." Andrei Sakharov, the physicist and dissident, spoke of the "regeneration" of Soviet society on a new moral foundation. "Corrupting lies, silence, and hypocrisy" could, he believed, be banished forever. This was not just an elite view. Polling done across the U.S.S.R. in 1989 found no deep, atavistic longing for a dictatorship. On the contrary, nine out of ten people said it was important for citizens to "express themselves freely." They acted on this belief: in the late 1980s, people in the Soviet Union argued about everything. I can remember little knots of people gathered in public parks, arguing and debating. Everyone felt that something momentous was happening, and some believed it would be good.

After the Soviet Union broke up, in 1991, the idea of *Wandel durch Handel*—"change through trade"—gained traction in Russia too. Reformers believed that deep and rapid engagement with the outside world would help them break up the old, dysfunctional system of central planning and create a new political as well as a new economic order. "I was absolutely sure that we will succeed," said Yegor Gaidar, the Russian economist who promoted the policy of "shock therapy." "I was absolutely sure that there is no other way, and absolutely sure that a delay is suicide for the country." But others had different plans.

Among them was Vladimir Putin. In a short documentary made in February 1992, Putin, then the deputy mayor of St. Petersburg, also argued in favor of small businesses. "The entrepreneurial class should become the basis for the flourishing of our society as a whole," he said. With what appeared to be true conviction, he encouraged Western partners to invest in Russian industry. Decades later, the director of that documentary, Igor Shadkhan, told the journalist Catherine Belton that Putin "really recruited me." He seemed, said Shadkhan, like a man "who would drive the country forward, who would really do something."

After he was named president, Putin did indeed drive the country in a new direction. Like the liberal economists, he wanted to reform the Soviet economic system, and hoped that Russia could become rich. But he remained nostalgic for the Soviet Empire, whose collapse he described as a "geopolitical disaster," and he certainly did not want to regenerate Soviet society on a new moral foundation. Karen Dawisha, author of one of the first books to describe Putin's political project in detail, observed that many mistakenly described Russia in the 1990s as "an inchoate democratic system being pulled down by history, accidental autocrats, popular inertia, bureaucratic incompetence, or poor Western advice." The real story of that decade was very different: "From the beginning, Putin and his circle sought to create an authoritarian regime ruled by a close-knit cabal . . . who used democracy for decoration rather than direction."

The state that finally emerged in the middle of the first decade of the twenty-first century was no longer a superpower. But Russia remained influential, more so than many understood at the time, as the model and inspiration for many other modern dictatorships. Putin's Russia was not an old-fashioned totalitarian state, isolated and autarkic. Nor was it a poor dictatorship, wholly dependent on foreign donors. Instead, it represented something new: a full-blown autocratic kleptocracy, a mafia state built and managed entirely for the purpose of enriching its leaders.

This project was launched much earlier than most understood. The first glimmer of the idea probably emerged in the Dresden headquarters of the KGB, where Putin was stationed in the 1980s and where KGB and Stasi teams were already building their network of spies, safe houses, and secret bank accounts. They were not alone: Russian "capitalism" was, from the very beginning, designed to favor insiders who knew how to extract and hide money abroad. No "level playing field" was ever created in Russia, and the power of competitive markets was never unleashed. Nobody became rich by building a better mousetrap. Those who succeeded did so thanks to favors granted by—or stolen from—the state. These were the true beneficiaries of this system: the oligarchs whose fortunes depended on their political connections.

By 1992, the year Shadkhan interviewed the future Russian president, Putin was already the executor and probably the prime beneficiary of a scheme designed to steal money from the city of St. Petersburg. His original swindle has now been investigated and described many times—inside Russia, initially, by the St. Petersburg City Council; outside Russia, by Dawisha, Belton, Masha Gessen, and others—and it was relatively straightforward. In his role as deputy mayor, Putin issued export licenses for raw materials such as diesel fuel, cement, and fertilizer. These shipments, purchased at low state prices in Russia, were meant to be sold at higher prices abroad in order to purchase food. The goods were indeed sold, but the money disappeared, diverted into the bank accounts of an obscure group of companies owned by Putin's friends and colleagues.

More complex schemes soon followed. They involved property in Russia, shell companies in Spain, Russian-Finnish joint ventures, German cutouts, and bank accounts in many different countries, probably including accounts that had been created years earlier. Like the St. Petersburg food swindle, the story of these investments and schemes has been told before. But usually, the emphasis is on the Russian actors and the Russian victims. Here I would like to draw attention to an aspect of Putin's origin story that is mentioned less frequently: the role of the legitimate Western institutions, companies, lawyers, and politicians who enabled his schemes, profited from them, or covered them up. The deputy mayor of St. Petersburg made his money thanks to the Western companies that bought the exports, the Western regulators who were unbothered by the bad contracts, and the Western banks that were strangely lacking in curiosity about the new streams of cash flowing into their accounts.

The same was true of another famous scheme, also dating from 1992, the year that Putin and a group of colleagues and partners from Russia, Germany, and Liechtenstein registered the St. Petersburg Real Estate Holding Company in Frankfurt. In 1998, the company went public on the Frankfurt

Stock Exchange, with Putin listed as a member of the advisory board. In 1999, the German Federal Intelligence Service published a report alleging that the company was laundering Russian money as well as international drug money. In 2000, just after Putin's inauguration as president of Russia, police in Liechtenstein arrested Rudolf Ritter, one of Putin's original partners. At that point the investigation seemed to slow down. Only in 2003 did police finally raid the twenty-seven offices and banks linked to the St. Petersburg Real Estate Holding Company in Germany. No charges against Putin were ever filed.

From the beginning of this story to the end, Western cooperation was essential. The money-laundering operation required the participation, among many others, of Ritter, who happened to be the brother of Liechtenstein's economy minister; of the other partners from Germany and Liechtenstein, along with their lawyers and accountants; of the officials at the Frankfurt Stock Exchange; and even of the German chancellor, Gerhard Schröder—the same one who was so certain trade would bring political change to China. Allegedly (although he later denied it), Schröder kept Putin informed about the investigation, in the name of peace, prosperity, and *Wandel durch Handel.*

The political system that eventually became Putinist Russia was the product of two worlds: the milieu of the KGB, on the one hand, with its long expertise in money laundering, gained from years of funding terrorists and sleeper agents, and the equally cynical, amoral world of international finance, on the other. Even as Western political leaders spoke about "democracy" and "rule of law" in Russia, Western companies and financial institutions were helping build autocracy and lawlessness, and not only in Russia. Before the British handed Hong Kong back to China, some British and other foreign businessmen were less than enthusiastic about democratic reforms in the colony, because they were hoping to establish relationships with the new regime. Chris Patten has written that even some British civil servants felt the same way.

By the time Putin became president, he was well acquainted with the double standards of Western democracies, which preached liberal values at home but were very happy to help build illiberal regimes everywhere else. In his first decade in office, he did the same, using the slogans of democracy, even as he built what eventually became a dictatorship. In an address to the nation in 2000, he declared that "only a democratic state is capable of ensuring a balance of interests of the individual and society, combining private initiative with national goals." In 2002, he said that a democratic state must have "rule of law, free elections, and the priority of human rights."

But although Russia was designed to *look* like a democracy, or at least enough like a democracy to fool foreign investors, there were no accidental victors in Russian elections, because there were no accidental candidates. The semblance of choice was carefully preserved through the emergence of regime-sanctioned opponents who never challenged the status quo. Meanwhile, genuine opponents of the Kremlin were beaten up at demonstrations, jailed, harassed, and insulted. In 2013, Alexei Navalny, who eventually became Putin's most effective critic, was allowed to run for mayor of Moscow in order to give a veneer of legitimacy to the race, but he attracted too much support. During that campaign he was convicted on fake charges of corruption; immediately afterward, he was placed under house arrest.

Russian capitalism was no different. Banks looked like banks, but they were not banks; they were just as often money-laundering operations. Companies looked like companies, but they too could be facades, vehicles for the very wealthy to siphon assets away from the state. Even for real companies, the market operated within limits: if the Kremlin decided to destroy a company, it could, and sometimes did. In 2004, Mikhail Khodorkovsky, the chairman of the oil company Yukos and at the time Russia's richest man, was arrested and sentenced to prison. Khodorkovsky spent the next decade in a labor camp. Yukos was driven into bankruptcy and sold at auction to a previously unknown purchaser whose company shared its address with a mobile phone shop in the city of Tver, northwest of Moscow. A few days later, the mystery company sold Yukos to Rosneft, an oil company whose majority shareholder was the Russian government. The CEO of Rosneft was also Putin's deputy chief of staff.

In due course, Rosneft was floated on the London Stock Exchange, backed by some of the most prestigious names in the financial world. Because nearly three-quarters of Rosneft's $80 billion value had been built on stolen assets, ABN AMRO Rothschild, Dresdner Kleinwort Wasserstein, J. P. Morgan, and Morgan Stanley—along with Linklaters (Rosneft's lawyers) and Ernst & Young (Rosneft's accountants)—did have to make the circumstances very clear. "Crime and corruption could create a difficult business climate in Russia," the prospectus noted. In case anybody was in doubt about who owned the company, the prospectus stated that the majority of the company would continue to be controlled by government officials, people "whose interests may not coincide with those of other shareholders . . . and may cause Rosneft to engage in business practices that do not maximise shareholder value." Nevertheless, these companies were said to have earned more than $100 million from the sale.

Duly warned, London investors bought up the shares anyway. Not long after the sale, in July 2006, the G8—the original G7 group of the seven wealthiest democracies, plus Russia—gathered in a lavishly renovated czarist palace just outside St. Petersburg. Putin was the host. At a press conference held during that summit, he declared that all the work he was doing was intended to make "this process of democratization and setting up the market economy irreversible in the Russian Federation. It is also aimed at putting in place the conditions required for the Russian people to make their own free choice."

Surely, Putin knew this wasn't true. Presumably, the journalists in the audience knew it wasn't true, and most probably the other presidents and prime ministers at the summit knew it wasn't true. And yet few objected, not least because so many inhabitants of the democratic world profited by accepting this fiction.

—

In 2010, things started going wrong at the steel plant in Warren, Ohio, a Rust Belt town that would later cast its votes twice for Donald Trump. A cooling panel started leaking, and the furnace operator didn't see the leak in time; the water hit molten steel, leading to an explosion that sent workers to the hospital with burns and other injuries. A year later, another explosion caused another round of destruction. A federal regulatory investigation turned up dozens of safety violations. "They just kept cutting corners," one employee said. "They were running a skeleton crew. They would not hire more help." A few years later, the plant halted operations. In January 2016, it shut down for good. Some two hundred people lost their jobs.

Here is how Casey Michel, the author of *American Kleptocracy,* described the Warren Steel plant in 2021:

> Cavernous holes gouge the siding, with peeling yellow and blue paint giving way to swaths of rust and sloshes of mud. Vacant lots and missing windows, crumpled cabinets and offices in disarray—whether trashed by looters or former employees is unclear—round out the place. The mill sits like something out of a dystopic future—or like something out of certain parts of the former Soviet Union.

Michel chose his words well, because the mill actually *was* "something out of certain parts of the former Soviet Union." At the time of its demise, Warren Steel was owned by Ihor Kolomoisky, a Ukrainian oligarch who gained his wealth during the era when Ukraine, like much of the rest of the post-Soviet world, was following the Russian path toward dictatorship and kleptocracy. According to the U.S. Department of Justice, Kolomoisky bought the mill, along with hundreds of millions of dollars' worth of other midwestern properties, as part of a money-laundering operation connected to the defrauding of PrivatBank, a retail bank in Ukraine. The oligarch probably needed to move cash that had been obtained illegally into something "real" in order to hide its origins (and perhaps in order to use it as collateral for legitimate loans). Kolomoisky might also have hoped that the towns and factories of the American Rust Belt were so desperate for cash that the origins of his money would be overlooked.

He might have been right. For decades, American real estate agents were not required to examine the source of their clients' funding the way that bankers and other businessmen do. It has long been possible, in the United States as in many European countries, to buy property anonymously, through shell companies. One in five condos in Trump-owned or Trump-branded buildings is owned anonymously, just to take one relevant example. Perhaps not all these mystery owners are money launderers, but if they were, we would never know. At least thirteen people with proven or alleged links to the Russian mafia are known to have owned or done business in condos in Trump-branded properties. Yet even while he was president of the United States, companies with mystery owners were still buying property in Trump's buildings; if that was a form of campaign contribution, we will never know.

During Kolomoisky's decade-long buying spree, from 2006 to 2016, companies linked to him acquired half a dozen steel mills, four office buildings, a hotel and conference center in Cleveland, an office park in Dallas, and a mothballed Motorola factory near Chicago. But few of the people living or working in these properties would have had any idea who he was, or that the money originally came from PrivatBank, because money for the purchases flowed into the Midwest via shell companies in Cyprus, the British Virgin Islands, and Delaware, with the assistance of the American arm of Deutsche Bank, traveling the same kind of route that Russian money, Kazakh money, Azeri money, Chinese money, Angolan money, or Venezuelan money also follows on its way out of kleptocratic autocracies and into markets and financial institutions in North America and Europe. Kolomoisky, who denies any wrongdoing (and is still fighting the nationalization of PrivatBank in Ukrainian and European courts), is hardly a household name in Cleveland.

In truth, his scheme was spoiled not by any American investigation but by Ukraine's 2014 Euromaidan revolution—the same street demonstrations that persuaded the pro-Russian president of Ukraine, Viktor Yanukovych, to flee the country. The demonstrators who came to Kyiv's central square were calling both for democracy and for an end to the grand corruption that had engulfed their country. The two Ukrainian presidents who have followed, Petro Poroshenko and Volodymyr Zelensky, both tried to set Ukraine on a different path, among other things through the investigation of PrivatBank. But while their efforts have received a good deal of attention and justified criticism, the Americans who played a role in Kolomoisky's U.S. adventure have not.

On the contrary, when Americans condemn Russian, Ukrainian, or post-Soviet corruption, they rarely reckon with the role their fellow citizens have played, or are still playing, in enabling it. Chaim Schochet, of Miami, was twenty-three when he started buying Cleveland real estate on behalf of Kolomoisky. Mordechai Korf, another Miami businessman, became the CEO of Optima Specialty Steel, the company that held industrial property in the United States purchased with Kolomoisky's money. Both Korf and Schochet used the services of an American lawyer, Marc Kasowitz, who also represented Donald Trump during the investigation into his Russian links, among other legal battles. On their behalf, Kasowitz claimed that Korf and Schochet had no knowledge of wrongdoing by Kolomoisky.

Their alleged scheme took a long time to uncover, partly because many of their investments make no sense to anyone who buys properties in order to manage them well and turn a profit. Their scheme, like Trump's sales to mystery clients, makes sense only within the arcane world of international kleptocracy, an alternative universe whose rules are so clearly different from those of the everyday economy that observers have invented special names for it. The British journalist Oliver Bullough has called this universe "Moneyland," the title of his 2019 book. Tom Burgis, an investigative reporter for the *Financial Times,* has called it "Kleptopia," the title of his 2020 book. They and others have repeatedly pointed out that this separate domain, jointly created by the autocratic world and the international financial community, is very large and very rich. Anonymously owned shell companies and funds based in offshore tax havens like Jersey and the Cayman Islands hide what could be as much as 10 percent of global GDP. This is money that has been earned from narcotics operations, hidden from tax authorities, or, in the case of Kolomoisky, allegedly stolen from ordinary Ukrainians. In this world, theft is rewarded. Taxes are not paid. Law enforcement is impotent and underfunded. Regulation is something to be dodged.

Most citizens in the world's democracies are vaguely aware of this alternate universe, but they imagine it exists in faraway countries or on exotic tropical islands. They are wrong. In October 2021, the International Consortium of Investigative Journalists, a nonprofit that pulls together newspapers from around the world, published excerpts from the Pandora Papers, a large cache of documents detailing the operations of tax havens and the people who keep money in them. Among other things, the records made clear how much clandestine financial traffic goes not just through the Caribbean, but through the United States and Great Britain. Wealthy Nigerians secretly own £350 million worth of British property. The king of Jordan legally used shell companies to purchase homes in London and Ascot, England. The consortium's investigation also showed, for the first time in such an accessible manner, how Delaware, Nevada, South Dakota, and Wyoming—nice, normal American states, full of nice, normal Americans—have created financial instruments that nameless investors can use to hide their money from the world.

They often do so by moving into perfectly ordinary places, where no one expects to find them. In 2016, I visited friends in Bramley, Hampshire, a rural village with a pub, a medieval church, green lawns, and a country estate. The estate, called Beaurepaire Park, had recently been bought by Elena Baturina, the wife of Yuri Luzhkov, the former mayor of Moscow. Intrigued to learn that Russia's only female billionaire had decided to experience English country life, I looked up the house in the British Land Registry. Although the purchase price was there—£5.5 million, or about $7.9 million—I found no Russian names. The owner was something called Skymist Holdings Limited, the same obscure company that was paying for the extensive renovations. Had I not happened to know that the former mayor himself had been seen in the pub (and had his lawyer not written a threatening letter when I mentioned the purchase in *The Washington Post*), I might never have been able to establish for certain whose identity Skymist Holdings Limited actually concealed.

What is equally difficult for the residents of small English villages and ailing American factory towns to understand is that the new clients, new neighbors, or new landlords moving money into their communities might be doing so because of their connections to a state that practices repression and political violence. To stay in power, modern autocrats need to be able to take money and hide it without being bothered by political institutions that encourage transparency, accountability, or public debate. The money, in turn, helps them shore up the instruments of repression. That, along with his historical fever dreams, is why Putin so hated Ukrainian democracy activism, and why he was so enraged by the 2014 Ukrainian revolution: if a similar movement ever won power in Russia, he would be the first to go to jail.

Kleptocracy and autocracy go hand in hand, reinforcing each other but also undermining any other institutions that they touch. The real estate agents who don't ask too many questions in Sussex or Hampshire, the factory owners eager to unload failing businesses in Warren, the bankers in Sioux Falls happy to accept mystery deposits from mystery clients—all of them help undermine the rule of law in their own countries and around the world. The globalization of finance, the plethora of hiding places, and the benign tolerance that democracies have shown for foreign graft now give autocrats opportunities that few could have imagined a couple of decades ago.

11

Kleptocracy Metastasizes

PRESIDENT HUGO CHÁVEZ arrived in office in 1998 after a strident campaign for change. He wanted to change the constitution, even change the name of the country. The Republic of Venezuela, established forty years earlier, was the wealthiest country in South America and had been one of the strongest democracies. But like many oil states, Venezuela was nepotistic and corrupt, albeit in a familiar, old-fashioned way. Politicians were sometimes bribed; in return, they sometimes gave deals to their friends. When oil prices fell in the 1990s, these arrangements created real anger. Chávez, a lieutenant colonel in the Venezuelan army who had staged a failed coup d'état in 1992, recognized that anger and used it. After he was released from prison he won an election by running against the corrupt Republic of Venezuela. He promised to create a more honest Bolivarian Republic of Venezuela instead.

One year later—when he was still perceived as an agent of reform—the new Venezuelan president held a meeting with his chief of internal police, Jesús Urdaneta. The two men had met as young army cadets. Together, they had planned the coup d'état in 1992. Together, they were imprisoned when the coup failed. Urdaneta was considered part of the Chávez inner circle.

Urdaneta came to see Chávez because he had evidence that the new, allegedly revolutionary government was beginning to indulge in corrupt practices too. He told the president that several top officials in his government were padding invoices for government contracts, including the printing contract for Chávez's proposed new constitution. According to an account he gave years later, Urdaneta urged Chávez to put an end to such behavior. If he refused, he said, it would spread.

Chávez listened but said nothing. Then, a few weeks later, he abruptly asked for Urdaneta's resignation. Venezuela's Supreme Court quashed any investigation into corruption. As Urdaneta had predicted, the ruling elite did indeed get the message: *If you are loyal, you can steal.*

Like Putin, Chávez made a choice. No one forced him to turn Venezuela into a kleptocracy, and even his own intelligence chief was surprised when he did. Nor was he somehow compelled to accept kleptocratic practices because of culture, history, or the weight of precedent. On the contrary, if he had sided with Urdaneta and established an expectation of probity across the public sector, his popularity might have increased. His regime might have had a better shot at actually improving people's lives, which is what he said he wanted to do. Instead, like Putin, he made a different political calculation, one designed not to make his country prosperous but to keep himself permanently in power. He was betting that corrupt officials would prove more malleable than clean ones, and he was right.

In the years that followed, cronies of Chávez would support the president's drive to eliminate all forms of accountability and transparency, both because doing so helped them stay in power and because it protected them from scrutiny. Like Putin, Chávez slowly broke democratic institutions in Venezuela—the press, the courts, the civil service, various ombudsmen—even while proclaiming his belief in democracy. His supporters went along with that too. Over time, the state itself began to act like a criminal syndicate, a parasite stripping resources off its host. State employees, accomplices in this process, adopted a policy of *omertà:* say nothing about anything. Since everybody was breaking the law, nobody wanted to talk about it.

For the officials who took part, the windfall was extraordinary. During the fourteen years Chávez held power, Venezuela took in nearly $800 billion in oil-export revenues. Much of this money did indeed finance state welfare programs, the same programs that persuaded foreign admirers to see Chávez as a progressive hero. But hundreds of billions of dollars from Petróleos de Venezuela, S.A. (PDVSA), the state oil company, as well as other Venezuelan state companies, made its way into bank accounts around the world. In 2017, investigators found that officials at PDVSA had been hiding millions of stolen dollars at a Portuguese bank, Banco Espírito Santo. A 2021 investigation showed that Swiss banks were hiding $10 billion on behalf of officials working at Venezuelan state banks, electrical utilities, and other entities. In that same year, journalists uncovered a $2 billion Venezuelan oil company scam that had been processed through banks in the principality of Andorra. Other schemes, impossible to discover, are presumed to have been carried out via tax havens. Transparency Venezuela, a nonprofit that monitors corruption, has documented 127 cases of large-scale corruption connected to PDVSA alone, including 17 believed to involve more than $1 billion.

Theft from the oil industry wasn't the only source of illicit revenues for regime insiders. Even more important was a form of corruption that hadn't existed on the same scale in the past: the industry of currency exchange manipulation, created by the state's byzantine system of multiple currency prices. At first, these opportunities were open to everyone. Young Venezuelans studying abroad could apply for an allowance of cheap dollars, which they were meant to use to pay for their studies. Thousands of middle-class kids quickly figured out how to game this system, thus producing a boomlet of Venezuelans at English-language schools in and around Dublin. They were there to drink Guinness, learn a few phrases, and profit from the artificial exchange rates as best they could.

Others never left Venezuela, instead paying unscrupulous schools to produce paperwork suggesting that they had studied abroad. Cheap dollars could then be swapped on the black market for many more Venezuelan bolivars than it had cost to buy them, earning the student a few thousand dollars in profit. The journalist Francisco Toro calls this mass participation in fraud the "democratization of kleptocracy," although of course there were bigger fraudsters too. The truly well connected worked out how to claim tens or hundreds of millions of dollars to import spare parts, medical supplies, telecommunications equipment, chemicals, computers. If Venezuela needed to import anything, then someone would be generating the fake paper trails and making discreet payoffs, just to unlock access to cheap currency.

No one really knows how much was lost. In Caracas in 2020, I sat in a room full of people who debated exactly how much money the regime had stolen—*$200 billion? $600 billion?*—a parlor game that gets played in Moscow too. Jorge Giordani, a Marxist economist who was once Chávez's minister of economy and finance, has estimated that the total amount stolen before 2013, the year Chávez died, was perhaps $300 billion. The loss is visible in the landscape of Caracas. Scattered around the Venezuelan capital are many brand-new, completely empty apartment buildings whose existence is reportedly a side effect of money laundering. With nowhere else to put illicit cash, people are storing money in glass and concrete, hoping that real estate prices will someday rise again. The impact on the landscape spreads beyond Caracas: a Miami court has charged a network of Venezuelan officials with laundering $1.2 billion into property and other assets in Florida, and elsewhere, too. Investigations into that case and others involve law-enforcement agencies all over the world.

For a long time, the Venezuelan state hid these scams not just from the law but from the court of public opinion. Learning from the example of Putin's campaign to convince the world that he believed in democracy, Chávez persuaded people inside and outside the country that his Bolivarian revolution was good for ordinary people, and especially good for the poor. He attracted celebrities and admirers, especially on the far end of the European left. Back in 2007, Hans Modrow, the last communist prime minister of East Germany, told me that Chávez's "Bolivarian socialism" represented his greatest hope: he imagined that the same Marxist ideas that had driven East Germany into collapse might succeed, finally, in bringing prosperity to Latin America. Jeremy Corbyn, the far-left leader of the British Labour Party, boasted of his meetings with Chávez and once described his regime as an "inspiration to all of us fighting back against austerity and neoliberal economics."

These admirers were attracted by the anti-Americanism, the neo-Marxism, and the flamboyant, strongman populism of Chávez, the images created by propaganda. Perhaps some of them didn't know about the corruption. But if they did know, they didn't care. They ignored corruption and dismissed its significance, at least until it brought down the entire economy.

The decline began with the oil industry. The first blow came in 2002–3, when Chávez threw the industry into chaos, firing nineteen thousand oil workers when they went on strike, replacing experts with loyalists. Later, commodity prices declined; later still, the Trump administration put sanctions on the PDVSA, which accelerated the collapse. At about the same time, thanks to the currency exchange scams, Venezuela began to suffer from critical shortages of everything. Billions (or maybe tens of billions) of state funds had vanished, the country's foreign currency had disappeared into private offshore accounts, hyperinflation accelerated, and imported goods disappeared.

Eventually they reappeared, but only for some. When I was in Caracas in 2020, I saw hard-currency stores where people with access to dollars could buy Cheerios or Heinz ketchup. Meanwhile, people without dollars faced hunger and malnutrition if not outright starvation. The Catholic charity Caritas estimated in 2019 that 78 percent of Venezuelans ate less than they used to, and 41 percent went whole days without eating. Doctors in Venezuelan hospitals faced pressure not to list malnutrition as either a cause of illness or a cause of death. Susana Raffalli, a renowned expert on food security, told me that she had witnessed an extraordinary scene in one hospital: the parents of a child who had died from starvation tried to give Raffalli the corpse, because they were afraid that state officials would take it away and hide it. She also visited a rural region where children left school at midday to hunt for birds or iguanas to cook and eat for lunch.

Corruption, as it turned out, was not a minor side effect of the Bolivarian revolution. Corruption lay at the heart of the autocracy that had replaced democracy, and Venezuelans knew it. That was why, in the months after the death of Chávez in 2013 and the installation of Nicolás Maduro as president, a series of powerful demonstrations rippled across the country. It felt as if it should have been the end of the regime, and many people expected that it would be. Instead, this was the moment when Autocracy, Inc., stepped up to help.

—

How does a rogue state survive under sanctions? New sources of funding can help: drug trafficking, illegal mining, extortion, kidnapping, gasoline smuggling. At different times, different members of the Venezuelan elite have tried all these. Generals, former ministers, and officials of the security services have been suspected and indeed convicted of smuggling cocaine. The Colombian-Venezuelan border is now pockmarked by illegal and unregulated gold mines. Kidnapping remains an acknowledged hazard on the drive from the airport to central Caracas. My friends advised me to arrive in daylight.

But a state that is a member of Autocracy, Inc., also has other options. There are friends and trading partners to be found among other sanctioned states, and companies not just unbothered by corruption but happy to encourage it and to participate themselves. Even as North American, South American, and European firms began pulling out of Venezuela, scared away by instability and risk, Russian companies, acting at their own behest as well as on behalf of the state, stepped in to replace them. Rosneft, Gazprom, Lukoil, and TNK-BP (a joint Russian-British venture) all put money into Venezuelan oil, agriculture, even manufacturing. Subsidized Russian grain exports to Venezuela grew, replacing grain that had previously come from the United States and Canada. Gasoline exported from Russia became the only gasoline available in Venezuela. Arms and armaments worth some $4 billion made their way to Caracas as well, including 100,000 Kalashnikovs, 24 fighter jets, and 50 helicopters.

As international institutions grew wary of lending to Venezuela, China stepped up to replace them. At that time, China would lend money without conditions, meaning that it did not demand economic or other reforms in exchange. That allowed first Chávez, then his successor, Maduro, to postpone any kind of financial reckoning and to proceed with the policies that eventually destroyed the Venezuelan economy. By about 2013 or 2014, the Chinese did finally realize that some $30 billion in loans might never be paid back and that an astonishingly expensive, Chinese-backed high-speed railway meant to cross Venezuela's lightly populated southern plains would never be completed. Venezuelan contractors would sign agreements and then simply abscond with the money.

Since this form of corruption was apparently new even to Chinese investors, they began asking for policy changes. At one point, some Chinese officials, finally cottoning on to the importance of governance, held clandestine conversations with the Venezuelan opposition. But these concerns never prevented the Chinese from selling surveillance technology, crowd-control equipment, and riot gear to the Maduro government, along with water cannons, tear-gas guns, and enormous movable walls that could block people from joining crowds—all tools that helped prevent the opposition from winning power.

Like China, Cuba had both financial and ideological reasons to back Venezuela. From the beginning of the Chávez presidency, the two countries saw themselves linked by a common anti-American agenda. Venezuela furnished Cuba with subsidized Venezuelan oil. In return, the Cuban government provided Venezuela with soldiers, police officers, and security and intelligence experts—some to replace Venezuelans whom Chávez didn't trust—as well as sports coaches, doctors, and nurses. Cuban spies still help the Venezuelan regime suppress the dissent that periodically bubbles up in the military (soldiers' families are affected by the food shortages and general discontent too), and Cubans have also taught the Venezuelan regime how to use shortages to their advantage, distributing food rations to their supporters and punishing opponents by taking food rations away. Starvation and malnutrition, the Cubans had learned, could be political tools too.

The warm relationship between Venezuela and Turkey, by contrast, seems to have evolved not from ideology but from personal links between Recep Tayyip Erdoğan, the Turkish president, and Maduro. The two men share a dislike of democracy and anticorruption movements inside their own countries as well as a feeling that they are "disrespected" by established democracies around the world. On a visit to Caracas in 2018, Erdoğan declared that he and Maduro had both been insulted: "They sometimes call us the sultan, or dictator. . . . We do not pay attention to them." That sealed the friendship: Venezuela ducks sanctions, exports gold to Turkey, and receives food in exchange.

Still, none of Venezuela's foreign relationships are more improbable than the regime's close, deep ties to Iran. The two countries have little in common historically, geographically, or ideologically. The Islamic Republic is a theocracy; the Bolivarian Republic ostensibly promotes left-wing internationalism. What binds them is oil, anti-Americanism, opposition to their own democracy movements, and a shared need to learn the dark art of sanctions evasion. If most countries relate to one another on the basis of trade or sympathy, Venezuela and Iran relate to each other on the basis of shared grievance, as well as a shared interest in clandestine petroleum sales.

Since 2000, Iran has systematically increased its aid, first for Chávez and then Maduro. Iranians bought Venezuelan gold and sent food and gasoline in return. Iranians are believed to be advising Venezuela on repressive tactics against dissidents. Iranians helped Venezuela build a drone factory (apparently with mixed success) and have sent equipment and personnel to help repair Venezuelan oil refineries. The Venezuelans, for their part, might have helped launder money for Hezbollah, the Iran-backed terrorist group, and are believed to have provided passports for Hezbollah and Iranian officials as well.

Iran's efforts alone would have made a big difference to the Venezuelan regime. But Iran plus Russia, China, Cuba, and Turkey have kept the profoundly unpopular Venezuelan regime afloat and even allowed it to support autocrats elsewhere. In October 2022, five Russian and two Spanish oil traders were indicted in the United States for participating in an elaborate conspiracy to simultaneously sidestep U.S. sanctions on the Venezuelan oil industry and evade the ban on exports of electronics and other technology to Russia. Using a complex web of shell companies—the same kinds of shell companies that are used to obscure ownership all over the democratic world—the seven traders conspired to send Venezuelan oil to buyers in China, obscuring its provenance. A U.S. Justice Department indictment alleges that the proceeds were used to buy high-tech components from U.S. companies for Russian military contractors, who used them to build weapons designed to kill Ukrainians.

This particular scheme was uncovered. How many more have not been? We know that others are still operating successfully in other autocracies, on other continents, with different participants speaking different languages but functioning in much the same way—for example, in Zimbabwe.

Uebert Angel is an evangelical pastor and British-Zimbabwean businessman who preaches the prosperity gospel: healing, prophecy, financial advice. On his website, he is shown wearing a white dinner jacket and a black bow tie. The site links to his various projects, among them the Millionaire Academy (which "teaches the fundamental aspects of becoming a millionaire") and a prophetic retreat (where, for a fee, participants will experience "physical, face-to-face time with the Prophet of God, the Prophet to Christianity, and to this Last Dispensation, Prophet Uebert Angel"). Why would people want to sign up? Because "this is the man Presidents around the world call to receive instruction; whom Millionaires and Billionaires in the world will fight over to meet in hopes of hearing a sentence that will raise the trajectory of their lives." He predicts volcanic eruptions, plane accidents, even victories for the Manchester United soccer team, broadcasting these prophecies on three YouTube channels—Miracle TV, Good-News TV, and Wow TV. He has also published a dozen-odd books, among them *How to Hear the Voice of God, Defeat-*

ing the Demon of Poverty, and *The Greatest Secret God Told Me About Money.* Like a magician, sometimes he even finds "miracle money"—gold, diamonds, and cash—in people's pockets or bank accounts.

In March 2023, another side of Uebert Angel was revealed when he appeared, unwittingly, in a four-part Al Jazeera documentary called *Gold Mafia.* The film described a series of overlapping gold-smuggling schemes, some of them closely allied with Zimbabwe's ruling party and its president, Emmerson Mnangagwa. One set of operations used old-fashioned human couriers, relying on payoffs to airport officials to get them to look the other way while gold bars were smuggled in hand luggage to Dubai. The gold belongs either to people who have stolen it or to people who cannot legally sell it because of international sanctions. Angel, who was taped by journalists who he thought were employees of a Chinese billionaire, appears in a slightly different role. Having been appointed Zimbabwe's "ambassador at large," allegedly to help bring investment and trade into Zimbabwe, he sells his diplomatic immunity to facilitate a classic "laundromat." Money obtained from gold sales is transferred to the bank accounts of criminal groups; they then hand over an equivalent amount of "dirty" money to the Zimbabwean government. (Through a spokesman, Angel called the documentary "misinformation, speculation, and deliberate efforts to scandalise the Presidential Envoy and Ambassador at Large, H. E. Ambassador Uebert Angel.")

Angel's personal assistant is another evangelical pastor, Rikki Doolan—who is white, British, and, judging by his

Twitter account, a part-time conservative culture warrior and campaigner against Pride marches. Pastor Rikki—also filmed secretly—says on camera that President Mnangagwa will ensure the scheme doesn't fail: "As long as you grease the wheels in Africa, there is no issue." He offers the Al Jazeera journalist (whom, again, he believes to be working for a Chinese billionaire) a meeting with the president. All he asks, in return, is a $200,000 "facilitation fee" to set it up. (In a video released after the scandal broke, Doolan said the documentary was the work of "imperialist-funded affiliates of Al-Jazeera" that had been "brutally edited to portray a false narrative.")

Alongside Angel and Doolan the film features an impressively diverse array of characters from all around Africa and the Middle East. Among them is a Dubai-based Canadian ("I can move as much as I want wherever I want for the most part. . . . The best thing with gold is it is cash"). Another is President Mnangagwa's niece, the head of Zimbabwe's mining association. A third is the head of a Kenyan political party who doubles as the owner of several gold-trading companies in Dubai and is also, as it happens, a pastor.

Their group business model is an ironic, inverse version of globalization: people from North America, southern Africa, Britain, and the United Arab Emirates happily coming together to collaborate across borders. Together, they evade sanctions and mutually profit, helped along by the lack of transparency in Zimbabwe and the repression of any political opposition.

They also represent something new. Political corruption

had been part of life in Zimbabwe—as in Venezuela and as in much of the developed world (think Tammany Hall)—for a very long time. After winning a war for independence from Britain, in 1980, the revolutionary leader Robert Mugabe built a classic one-party state. He and Mnangagwa, at the time his security chief, repressed and murdered their rivals and eventually ran the country as a sprawling patronage network. But in the 1980s there were no complex international transactions involved, no middlemen in Dubai. Most of the spoils—jobs, contracts, kickbacks—went to favored businessmen from Mugabe's Shona tribe. The origin of the money was old-fashioned too: for twenty years after independence, white-owned farms continued to produce the cash crops—mostly tobacco, but also sugar and cut flowers—that accounted for the bulk of Zimbabwe's exports.

This system was knocked sideways in 2002 by a long-promised, badly needed, and, in practice, chaotic and violent land reform. Mugabe expropriated many of the white farmers, handing much of the land to his supporters and excluding many former black farmworkers. Farm production collapsed; export revenues plunged. The central bank began to print money, and inflation rose. The government imposed currency controls, with the same result as in Venezuela: regime insiders learned to manipulate the system of multiple exchange rates. At the same time, mining replaced farming as the main source of hard currency, and this also helped well-connected Zimbabweans, who found gold easier to export and to sell "off the books" than tobacco or flowers.

But it wasn't just Zimbabwe that had changed. Financial systems around the world had accustomed themselves to kleptocratic cash. Between 1980 and 2002, new kinds of states emerged, not just tax havens, but "bridging jurisdictions," as a National Endowment for Democracy study calls them. These are hybrid states that are a legitimate part of the international financial system, that trade normally with the democratic world, that are sometimes part of democratic military alliances, but that are also willing to launder or accept criminal or stolen wealth or to assist people and companies that have been sanctioned. The United Arab Emirates, for example, has in recent years made it much easier for foreigners, even those under sanctions, to become residents or even citizens and to buy property. As a result, Russian property purchases in the Emirates rose 100 percent after the invasion of Ukraine. Turkey has also created loopholes that make it easier not just for Russians but for anyone to transfer money into the country and to import cash and gold directly. In addition to these open invitations to sanctioned foreigners, this trade has a clandestine face: gold smuggling into Dubai, for example, or the Turkish schemes to transport gold from Venezuela to Iran.

An influx of kleptocratic cash can also empower regimes to become more autocratic and repressive themselves. Starting in 2022, exports from Kyrgyzstan to Russia grew by two and a half times. The products that flowed from the central Asian republic included some that the Kyrgyz had never exported to Russia before: shampoo, toothpicks, soap, car parts, and other goods made in Europe or China, by European or Chinese companies that wanted to evade sanctions. At the same time, timber and wood products produced in Belarus also appeared in European markets labeled as Kyrgyz or Kazakh, neither of which had previously exported wood to Europe either. In the same two-year period, Kyrgyzstan's autocratic regime also grew harsher. Having previously permitted a relatively free press and open political conversation—one of the most open in the region—Kyrgyzstan began to ban publications and pass laws restricting reporters. The state confiscated journalists' phones and laptops, in some cases after accusing them of violating a vaguely worded law that bans "calls to disobedience and mass riots."

The shift was dramatic. In 2007, Bektour Iskender co-founded Kloop, a Kyrgyz investigative website that did serious reporting on corruption, trained young journalists, and cooperated closely with other central Asian publications. By 2020, Kloop was producing regular scoops and investigations, including a carefully researched, minutely detailed series of articles exposing a multimillion-dollar smuggling and money-laundering scheme in Kyrgyzstan. When I met him in the summer of 2022, Iskender was full of optimism and plans for cross-border and investigative projects. His TED Talk on "the crime fighting power of investigative journalism" was heard by 1.5 million people. When I met him for a second time eighteen months later, he was facing the prospect of long-term exile. Over coffee in Warsaw, he told me that he'd been warned to leave his country. The regime, he said, had been "emboldened by the huge influx of Russian money." The prospects for any positive change, whether more free speech or more transparency, were now very slim, given how much dirty money was suddenly available to preserve the status quo. By November 2023, Kyrgyzstan had blocked the Kloop websites in both the Russian and the Kyrgyz languages.

Over a decade, a similar shift took place in Zimbabwe. In 2008, the mismanagement created a true crisis: the inflation rate had topped 200 million percent, the largest Zimbabwean dollar notes had values in the trillions, and Mugabe seemed poised to make changes. A plausible opposition emerged, the Movement for Democratic Change. Its leader, Morgan Tsvangirai, actually won the first round of a presidential election. At that moment, Mugabe could have allowed a democratic transition to take place. He could have made way for a genuine economic reform, one designed to benefit all Zimbabweans, and not just the ruling party. He could have allowed space, at least, for an honest discussion of Zimbabwe's perpetual crisis. Instead, Mugabe responded with violence. Ruling party thugs harassed and beat up Tsvangirai's supporters. The Zimbabwe Human Rights Forum documented 137 political abductions or kidnappings, 19 disappearances, 107 murders, and 6 politically motivated rapes.

Instead of restoring the rights of Zimbabwe's citizens, instead of seeking general prosperity, Mugabe and his inner circle took advantage of opportunities that had not been available back in 1980. They morphed from "traditional" corrupt leaders into something else: a new class of oligarchs whose money was hidden behind a blizzard of transactions that most Zimbabweans find impossible to understand. In a country where some people can become fabulously rich just by being in the right place at the right time while others remain poor, it is no wonder Uebert Angel's financial advice and "miracle money" attract so much faith and hope: a form of invisible foreign "magic" has made a few people extremely wealthy. Maybe a different form of magic could help others?

But precisely because magical wealth was not available to everyone, the leadership also had to find new ways of controlling popular unrest. After Mnangagwa pushed out Mugabe in 2017, he began to shut down whatever elements of the rule of law remained in Zimbabwe. He assaulted the court system, amending the constitution in 2021 to give himself the power to hire and fire judges, and distributed bribes, disguised as housing loans, to keep judges friendly.

In the run-up to elections in August 2023, he pushed through the "Patriotic Bill," a law that, in effect, made it a crime for any Zimbabwean to say anything negative about Zimbabwe or its government to any foreigner. I had planned to go to Zimbabwe to observe those elections, but after the bill passed I canceled the trip. Instead, I talked to several opposition candidates by telephone during the campaign. They were enthusiastic, organized, and motivated. Dislike of the regime was widespread, they told me, and they were sure they had a chance to win.

A few days later, after the election was rigged to ensure another government victory, one of them called me in a panic to ask if I could help him escape the country. Police in his district were arresting his colleagues. The violence and the corruption brought more U.S. and EU sanctions, including some against individual perpetrators. But just as the international financial system had created many services that could help them make and hide their money, the Zimbabwean elite knew, by 2023, that it had alternatives.

The ruling party had a long-standing relationship with the Chinese Communist Party, dating back to the days when they shared Maoist slogans and talked of peasant rebellion. The Chinese had provided weapons, training, and advice to Mugabe's Zanu-PF party back when they were still fighting for independence, and later during the struggle against a rival liberation party backed by the Soviet Union. After independence, China slowly became the largest investor in Zimbabwe, the largest source of imports, and an important destination for exports. By 2022, Chinese aid had contributed to a wide range of projects, from a national pharmaceutical warehouse to Zimbabwe's new parliament building. During the pandemic, China gave Zimbabwe a million doses of its Sinovac COVID-19 vaccine.

The mutual interest was clear. China got minerals: in September 2022, Chinese investors signed a $2.8 billion deal to build processing facilities for lithium, platinum, and nickel for export to Chinese battery factories. In exchange, Zimbabwe got broadband deals and Chinese surveillance technology, including Huawei equipment and surveillance cameras that China has long used to track internal dissent. Other Chinese technology firms, including some that produce facial-recognition software, signed deals to provide equipment for what was vaguely described as "law enforcement purposes." Zimbabwe turned over its telecommunications infrastructure to China. In return, China helped Mnangagwa stay in power.

Although there is no deep, historic link between Harare and Moscow, Mnangagwa and Putin eventually discovered they had much in common too. Both men stay in power not through elections or constitutions but through propaganda, corruption, and selective violence. Both need to show audiences at home and in the democratic world how little they care about their criticism, their human rights laws, their talk of democracy. In order to demonstrate solidarity with Russian kleptocracy, Zimbabwe became one of eleven countries to vote at the United Nations in favor of the Russian annexation of Crimea in 2014, along with North Korea, Belarus, Cuba, and Venezuela. That same year, Zimbabwe handed Russia a platinum-mining concession and obtained several MiG-35 fighter jets in exchange. In 2019, Putin welcomed Mnangagwa to Moscow a week after Mnangagwa's police had fired on protesters in Harare. They signed agreements on Russian investment in Zimbabwe's diamond industry.

In 2023, their relationship reached a new plateau when Mnangagwa, the former leader of an anticolonial independence movement, offered his support for Putin's brutal war of colonial domination in Ukraine. Zimbabwe, he declared at a Russia-Africa summit in St. Petersburg, "is in solidarity with the Russian Federation in your country's special military operation in Ukraine." A grateful Putin offered his new comrade the gift of a presidential helicopter. "This bird will soon be gracing our skies," the Zimbabwean government spokesman proclaimed. He published a photograph of the octogenarian Mnangagwa sitting in the helicopter's cabin beside a table laden with wine and fruits, and Mnangagwa's statement to the Zimbabwean people and to the world. "The victims of sanctions must cooperate," he said.

III

Controlling the Narrative

On June 4, 1989, the Polish Communist Party held partially free elections, setting into motion a series of events that ultimately removed the communists from power. Not long afterward, street demonstrations calling for free speech, accountability, and democracy helped bring down communist regimes in East Germany, Czechoslovakia, Hungary, and Romania. Within a few years, the Soviet Union itself ceased to exist.

Also on June 4, 1989, the Chinese Communist Party ordered the military to remove thousands of students from Tiananmen Square. Like the East Europeans, they were calling for free speech, accountability, and democracy. But soldiers arrested and killed demonstrators in Beijing and around the country, then tracked down the leaders of the protest movement and forced them to confess and recant. Some spent years in jail. Others managed to elude their pursuers and flee the country forever.

In the aftermath of these events, the Chinese concluded

that even this response was insufficient. To prevent the democratic wave then sweeping across Western Europe from spreading to the East, China's leaders set out to eliminate not just the people but the *ideas* that had motivated the protests: the rule of law, the separation of powers, the right to freedom of speech and assembly, and all the principles that they described as "spiritual pollution" coming from the democratic world. Well before Xi Jinping set China on the path to one-man rule, the Chinese began using new information technologies that were just then beginning to change politics and conversations around the world.

Even as this system was under construction, nobody believed that it would work. If Americans were naive about the role that trade would play in building democracy, they were even more starry-eyed about technology. It's worth remembering again that room full of foreign policy experts who laughed, back in 2000, when President Clinton said that any Chinese attempt to control the internet would be like "trying to nail jello to the wall." Books with titles like *Here Comes Everybody* and *Virtuous Reality* once argued that the internet would lead to a boom in self-organization, even a cultural renaissance. As recently as 2012, it was still possible for a reviewer in *The New York Times* to belittle the idea, expressed in a book of mine, that the internet could become a tool of control. "Vladimir Putin may yet make her a prophet," wrote Max Frankel about me, "but so far this century, technology has become a welcome defense against tyranny."

While we were still rhapsodizing about the many ways in which the internet would spread democracy, the Chinese were designing the system sometimes known as the Great Firewall of China. That name, despite its pleasing historical echo, is misleading. "Firewall" sounds like a physical object, and China's system of internet management—in fact, conversation management—contains many different elements, beginning with an elaborate system of blocks and filters that prevent internet users from seeing particular words and phrases. Among them, famously, are the words "Tiananmen," "1989," and "June 4," but there are many more. In 2000, something called the Measures for Managing Internet Comment Provision prohibited an extraordinarily wide range of content, including anything that "endangers national security, divulges state secrets, subverts the government, undermines national unification," and "is detrimental to the honor and interests of the state"—anything, in other words, that the authorities don't like. Chinese social media was allowed to flourish, but only in cooperation with the security services, which engineered it from the beginning to enable the surveillance of users.

Foreign companies helped, initially rushing into this new security market the same way they had rushed into post-Soviet financial markets. Microsoft at one point altered its blogging software to accommodate the Great Firewall's protocols. Yahoo agreed to sign a "public pledge on self-discipline," ensuring that forbidden terms wouldn't turn up in its searches. Cisco Systems, another U.S. company, sold hundreds of millions of dollars of equipment to China, including technology that blocked traffic to banned websites. When I wrote about these sales in 2005, a spokesman told me this was the "same equipment technology that your local library uses to block pornography," adding, "We're not doing anything illegal." Harry Wu, the late Chinese human rights activist, told me he had learned from Cisco representatives in China that the company had contracts to provide technology to the police departments of at least thirty-one provinces.

But as in so many other spheres, China absorbed the technology it needed and then eased the foreign companies out. Google struggled to adhere to the Great Firewall's rules before giving up in 2010, following a cyberattack orchestrated by the People's Liberation Army. The company later worked secretly on a version of its search engine that would be compatible with Chinese censorship, but abandoned that as well, following staff protest and public criticism in 2018. China banned Facebook in 2009 and Instagram in 2014. TikTok, although invented by a Chinese company, has never been permitted to function in China at all.

The Chinese regime also cast the net wider, beyond cyberspace, learning to combine online tracking systems with other tools of repression, including security cameras, police inspections, and arrests. The most sophisticated version of this combined system now operates in Xinjiang, the province inhabited by China's minority Muslim Uighur population. Following a series of political protests there in 2009, the state began not only to arrest and detain Uighurs but also to experiment with new forms of online and offline control. Uighurs have been required to install "nanny apps" on their phones, which constantly search for "ideological viruses," including Koranic verses and religious references as well as suspicious statements in all forms of correspondence. The apps can monitor purchases of digital books and track an individual's location, sending the information back to police. They can also pick up unusual behavior: anyone who downloads a virtual private network, anyone who stays off-line altogether, and anyone whose home uses too much electricity (which could be evidence of a secret houseguest) can arouse suspicion. Voice-recognition technology and even DNA swabs are used to monitor where Uighurs walk, drive, and shop.

Eventually, this system could spread across all of China, where hundreds of millions of security cameras already monitor public spaces. Artificial intelligence and facial-recognition software already identify people who walk past the cameras, instantly linking them to other information picked up from phones, social media, and other sources. A so-called social credit system already connects a wealth of databases, blacklisting individuals who break the rules. Sometimes this system is described by the benign term "safe city technology," as if its only purpose were to improve traffic flows, and indeed it does that too.

Safety is hardly the only goal. The tech journalist Ross Andersen has written in *The Atlantic* that soon "Chinese algorithms will be able to string together data points from a broad range of sources—travel records, friends and associates, reading habits, purchases—to predict political resistance before it happens." With every new breakthrough, with every AI advance, China gets closer to its version of the holy grail: a system that can eliminate not just the words "democracy" and "Tiananmen" from the internet but the thinking that leads people to become democracy activists or attend public protests in real life.

Other countries could follow suit. "Safe city technology," surveillance, and AI systems have been sold by the Chinese tech behemoth Huawei to Pakistan, Brazil, Mexico, Serbia, South Africa, and Turkey. One branch of the Malaysian security services closed a deal with a Chinese company whose AI technology will help it compare camera images, in real time, with images in a central database. Singapore has acquired a similar range of products, even announcing plans to put cameras enabled with facial-recognition technology on every lamppost in the city-state. President Mnangagwa bought facial-recognition technology for Zimbabwe, supposedly for the purpose of designing "intelligent security applications at airports, and railway and bus stations" but with clear potential for political control as well.

It's a matter of time before these ideas spread further, tempting the leaders of democracies too. Some elements of "safe city technology" really can help combat crime, and plenty of democracies experiment with it. Democracies, especially hybrid democracies, are also perfectly capable of deploying their own surveillance technology, using it against critics and political opponents as well as genuine criminals or terrorists. Pegasus mobile phone spyware, created by the Israeli company NSO, has been used to track journalists, activists, and political opponents in Hungary, Kazakhstan, Mexico, India, Bahrain, and Greece, among others. In 2022, the Polish government at the time, led by the national-populist Law and Justice Party, put Pegasus software on the phones of friends and colleagues of mine, all of whom were affiliated with what was then the political opposition. Debate over what information the American government should and should not retain about American citizens became, in 2013, the subject of an international scandal when Edward Snowden, a contractor for the National Security Agency (NSA), revealed the NSA's methods and tactics and at the same time published thousands of documents detailing American military operations around the world. Snowden fled to Russia, where he remains.

There are important differences between the way these stories play out in democracies and dictatorships. Snowden's leaks were widely discussed. Journalists won Pulitzer Prizes for investigating them. In Poland, the Pegasus spyware scandal was eventually exposed and investigated, first by the media and later by a parliamentary committee. If no parallel scandal has ever unfolded in China, Russia, Iran, or North Korea, that's because there are no legislative committees or free media that could play the same role.

Still, the democratic world's use of spyware and surveillance does help the autocracies justify their own abuse of these technologies. As more countries adopt these systems, the ethical and moral objections will fade. China exports these technologies for commercial reasons, possibly for espionage, but also because their spread justifies their use at home: if there are fewer objections to mass surveillance outside China, then there is less danger that criticism will be heard inside China. Dictators, political parties, and elites who have come to depend upon advanced Chinese technology to control their populations may also begin to feel some obligation to align themselves with China politically, or maybe even the necessity to do so, in order to stay in power. The more China can "bring other countries' models of governance into line with China's own," argues Steven Feldstein, an expert in digital technology, "the less those countries pose a threat to Chinese hegemony."

Yet even the most sophisticated forms of surveillance provide no guarantees. During the years of the pandemic, the Chinese government imposed the most severe controls on physical movement that most Chinese had ever experienced. Millions of people were forced or even locked into their homes; untold numbers of people entered government quarantine camps. Nevertheless, the lockdown also produced the angriest and most energetic Chinese protests in many years. Young people who had never attended a demonstration and had no memory of Tiananmen gathered in the streets of Beijing and Shanghai in the autumn of 2022 to talk about freedom of movement and freedom of speech. In Xinjiang, where lockdowns were the longest and harshest in all of China, and where internet controls are the deepest and most complete, people came out in public and sang the Chinese national anthem, emphasizing one line of the lyrics: "Rise up, those who refuse to be slaves!" Clips of their performance circulated widely, because the spyware and filters didn't identify the national anthem as dissent.

The lesson for Autocracy, Inc., was ominous: even in a state where surveillance seems total, the experience of tyranny and injustice can always radicalize people. Anger at arbitrary power will always lead someone to start thinking about some other system, some better way to run society. The strength of these demonstrations and the broader anger they reflected were enough to spook the Chinese authorities into lifting the quarantines and allowing the virus to spread. The deaths that resulted were preferable to public anger and protest.

Broader lessons might have been drawn too. Like the anti-Putin demonstrations in Russia in 2011, or the huge street protests in Caracas a few years later, the 2022 protests in China would have given autocratic regimes another reason to turn their repressive mechanisms outward, into the democratic world. If people are naturally drawn to the image of human rights, to the language of democracy, to the dream of freedom, then those ideas have to be poisoned. That requires not just surveillance, and not merely a political system that defends against liberal ideas. It also requires an offensive plan, a narrative that damages the idea of democracy, wherever it is being used, anywhere in the world.

In the twentieth century, Communist Party propaganda was overwhelming and inspiring, or at least it was meant to be. Posters, art, movies, and newspapers portrayed a shiny and idealized future, filled with clean factories, abundant produce, enthusiastic workers, and healthy tractor drivers. The architecture was designed to overpower, the music to intimidate, the public spectacles to produce awe. In theory, citizens were meant to feel enthusiasm, inspiration, and hope.

In practice, this kind of propaganda backfired, since people could compare what they saw in posters and movies with a far more impoverished reality.

A few autocracies still portray themselves to their citizens as model states. The North Koreans, famously, hold vast military parades with elaborate gymnastics displays and huge portraits of their leader, very much in the Stalinist style. But many of the propagandists of Autocracy, Inc., have learned from the mistakes of the twentieth century. They don't offer their fellow citizens a vision of utopia, and they don't inspire them to build a better world. Instead, they teach people to be cynical and passive, because there is no better world to build. Their goal is to persuade people to mind their own business, stay out of politics, and never hope for a democratic alternative: *Our state may be corrupt, but everyone else is corrupt too. You may not like our leader, but the others are worse. You may not like our society, but at least we are strong and the democratic world is weak, degenerate, divided, dying.*

Instead of portraying China as the perfect society, modern Chinese domestic propaganda seeks to inculcate nationalist pride, based on China's real experience of economic development and national redemption. The Chinese regime also draws a contrast between their own "order" and the chaos or violence of democracy. Chinese media mocked the laxity of the American response to the pandemic with an animated film that ended with the Statue of Liberty on an intravenous drip. Later, China's *Global Times* wrote that Chinese people were calling the January 6 insurrection "karma" and "retribution": "Seeing such scenarios, many Chinese will naturally recall that Nancy Pelosi once praised the violence of Hong Kong protesters as a 'beautiful sight to behold.'" (Pelosi, of course, had praised peaceful demonstrations, not violence.) The Chinese are also told that these forces of chaos are out to disrupt their own lives, and they are encouraged to fight against them in a "people's war" against foreign influence or foreign spies: "Foreign hostile forces have been working very hard, and [we] should never drop our guard on national security work."

Russians hear even less about what happens in their own towns or cities. Instead, they are told constantly about the decline of places they don't know and have mostly never visited: America, France, Britain, Sweden, Poland, countries apparently filled with degeneracy, hypocrisy, and Russophobia. A study of Russian television from 2014 to 2017 found that negative news about Europe appeared on the three main Russian channels, all state controlled, an average of eighteen times a day. Some of the stories were obviously invented (*European governments are stealing children from straight families and giving them to gay couples!*), but even true stories were cherry-picked to support the idea that daily life in Europe is frightening and chaotic, that Europeans are weak and immoral, and that the European Union is either dictatorial and interventionist or, alternatively, about to fall apart. The goal is clear: to prevent Russians from identifying with Europe, as Russians once did.

If anything, the portrayal of America has been more dramatic. Americans who rarely think about Russia would be stunned to learn how much time Russian state television devotes to America's culture wars, especially arguments over gender. Putin himself has displayed an alarmingly intimate acquaintance with Twitter debates about transgender rights, mockingly sympathizing with people who he says have been "canceled." In part this is to demonstrate to Russians that there is nothing to admire about the liberal democratic world. But this is also Putin's way of building alliances between his domestic audiences and his supporters in Europe and North America, where he has a following on the authoritarian far right, having convinced some naive conservatives that Russia is a "white Christian state." In reality, Russia has very low church attendance, legal abortion, and a multiethnic population containing millions of Muslim citizens. The autonomous region of Chechnya, which is part of the Russian Federation, is governed in part by elements of sharia law and has arrested and killed gay men in the name of Islamic purity. The Russian state harasses and represses many forms of religion outside the state-sanctioned Russian Orthodox Church, including evangelical Protestants.

Putin's portrayal of Russia as the leader of an alliance of strong, traditional states against weak democracies has nevertheless won some adherents in America. White nationalists marching in the infamous Charlottesville demonstration that ended in violence in 2017 shouted, among other slogans, "Russia is our friend." Russians participate in international organizations that purport to promote Christian or traditional values and are suspected of covertly funding some of them. Putin sends periodic messages to this constituency. "I uphold the traditional approach that a woman is a woman, a man is a man, a mother is a mother and a father is a father," he told a press conference in December 2023, almost as if this were a justification for the war in Ukraine. Just before that press conference, the Russian state banned what it called the "international LGBTQ+ movement" as a form of "extremism," and police began to raid gay bars.

This manipulation of the strong emotions about gay rights and feminism has been widely copied throughout the autocratic world. Yoweri Museveni, president of Uganda for more than three decades, also passed an "anti-homosexuality" bill in 2014, instituting a life sentence for gay couples who marry and criminalizing the "promotion" of a homosexual lifestyle. By picking a fight over gay rights, he was able to consolidate his supporters at home while neutralizing foreign criticisms of his regime. He accused the democracies of "social imperialism": "Outsiders cannot dictate to us; this is our country," he declared. Viktor Orbán, the prime minister of Hungary, an illiberal hybrid state, also ducks discussion of Hungarian corruption by hiding behind a culture war. He has adopted the pretense that ongoing tension between his government and the U.S. government concerns religion and gender, when in fact the poor relationship was created by Orbán's deep financial and political ties to Russia and China.

Other autocrats monopolize national conversations by accruing as much attention as possible for themselves. Hugo Chávez appeared on Venezuelan television constantly, preempting regular programming and dominating all television and radio channels at once. On Sundays he conducted an hours-long talk show, *Aló Presidente,* during which he treated viewers to long monologues on politics or sports, as well as personal anecdotes and songs. Sometimes he invited celebrities to join him, among them Naomi Campbell and Sean Penn. In some ways, his monopoly of the national conversation prefigured Donald Trump's 2016 election campaign, although Trump made use of social media, not television, to dominate the conversation. Both men also lied repeatedly, and blatantly, as do other modern dictators. The political scientist Lisa Wedeen has observed that the Syrian regime tells lies so ludicrous that no one could possibly believe them, for example that Syria, at the height of the civil war, was an excellent tourist destination. These "national fictions," she concluded, were meant not to persuade anyone, but rather to demonstrate the power of the people who were spinning the stories. Sometimes the point isn't to make people believe a lie; it's to make people fear the liar.

This too marks a departure from the past. Soviet leaders also lied, but they tried to make their falsehoods seem real. Like Khrushchev at the UN, they became angry when anyone accused them of lying, and in response they produced fake "evidence" or counterarguments. In Putin's Russia, Assad's Syria, or Maduro's Venezuela, politicians and television personalities often play a different game. They lie constantly, blatantly, obviously. But when they are exposed, they don't bother to offer counterarguments. When Russian-controlled forces shot down Malaysia Airlines Flight 17 over Ukraine in 2014, the Russian government reacted not only with a denial but with multiple stories, plausible and implausible: they blamed the Ukrainian army, or the CIA, or a nefarious plot in which 298 dead people were placed on a plane in order to fake a crash and discredit Russia.

This tactic, the so-called "fire hose of falsehoods" produces not outrage but nihilism. Given so many explanations, how can you know what actually happened? What if you can never know? If you can't understand what is going on around you, then you are not going to join a great movement for democracy, or follow a truth-telling leader, or listen when anyone speaks about positive political change. Instead, you will avoid politics altogether. Autocrats have an enormous incentive to spread that hopelessness and cynicism, not only in their own countries, but around the world.

At a dinner in Munich in February 2023, I found myself seated across the table from a European diplomat who had just returned from Africa. He had met with some students there and had been shocked to discover how little they knew or cared about the war in Ukraine. They had repeated Russian claims that the Ukrainians are "Nazis," blamed NATO for the invasion, and generally used the same kind of language that can be heard every night on Russian evening news. The diplomat was mystified. He grasped for explanations: Maybe it was a legacy of colonialism, or Western neglect of the Global South. Maybe this was just the long shadow of the Cold War. He shook his head.

Like so many Europeans and Americans who seek to explain the world using only their own experience, he had missed the simplest and most obvious explanation. The story of how Africans—as well as Latin Americans, many Asians, and indeed many Americans and Europeans—have come to repeat Russian propaganda about Ukraine is not primarily a story about European colonial history. It rather involves China's systematic efforts to buy or influence media and elite audiences around the world; carefully curated Russian propaganda campaigns, some amplified by both paid and unpaid members of the American and European far right; and, increasingly, the efforts of other autocracies piggybacking on these networks, using the same tactics and the same language to promote their own illiberal regimes, often for the purpose of achieving similar narrative control. Antidemocratic rhetoric has gone global.

Perhaps because it is the wealthiest autocracy, and perhaps because its leaders really do believe they have a good story to tell, China has made the greatest effort to present itself to the world, doing so in the largest number of countries and using the widest range of channels. The analyst Christopher Walker has coined the term "sharp power"—neither "hard" military power nor "soft" cultural power—to describe the Chinese influence campaigns that are now felt in many different areas of culture, media, academia, and even sports. Many are coordinated by the United Front, the Chinese Communist Party's most important influence project, which creates educational and exchange programs, seeks to control Chinese exile communities, builds Chinese chambers of commerce, and, most notoriously, helps run the Confucius Institutes, situated within academic institutions all over the world. Originally perceived as benign cultural bodies, not unlike the Goethe Institute run by the German government or the Alliance Française, the Confucius Institutes were welcomed by many universities because they provided cheap or even free Chinese-language classes and professors. Over time, the institutes aroused suspicion by policing Chinese students at American universities, seeking to block public discussions of Tibet or Taiwan, and in some cases altering the teaching of Chinese history and politics to suit Chinese narratives. Although mostly disbanded in the United States, Confucius Institutes flourish in many other places. There are several dozen in Africa alone.

These subtler operations are augmented by China's enormous investment, estimated at $7–10 billion, in international media. The Xinhua wire service, China Global Television Network (CGTN), China Radio International, and the China Daily web portal all receive significant state financing, have social media accounts in multiple languages and regions, and sell, share, or otherwise promote their content. Their news and video feeds are professionally produced, heavily subsidized, cost less than their Western equivalents, and always show China and Chinese allies in a positive light. Hundreds of news organizations in Europe, Asia, and Africa use their content, including many in Africa, from Kenya and Nigeria to Egypt and Zambia. Their regional hub is in Nairobi, where they hire prominent local journalists and produce content in African languages, in addition to Arabic, English, French, Spanish, Russian, and Chinese.

At the moment, not many people watch these Chinese-owned channels, whose output is predictable and often boring. But softer forms of Chinese television are gradually becoming available. StarTimes, a semiprivate, Chinese-linked satellite television company, now has more than thirteen million subscribers in thirty African countries. StarTimes is cheap for consumers, costing just a few dollars a month. It prioritizes Chinese content, not just news but kung fu movies, soap operas, and Chinese Super League football, with the dialogue and commentary all translated into Hausa, Swahili, and other African languages. Western content is available on the satellite, but costs extra. StarTimes has also acquired a stake in a South African satellite television company and created a partnership with a Zambian state broadcaster. In this way, even entertainment can carry China-positive messages.

Unlike much Western media, these outlets cooperate not just with one another but directly with the Chinese government. China doesn't separate propaganda, censorship, diplomacy, and media into separate compartments or think about them as separate activities, whether inside or outside China. Legal pressure on foreign news organizations, the blocking of foreign websites, online trolling operations aimed at foreign journalists, cyberattacks—all these can be deployed as part of a single operation designed to undermine a particular organization or to promote a particular narrative. The Chinese Communist Party uses student associations and trade groups to send messages, offers training courses or stipends for local journalists, even provides phones and laptops. This is also part of a clear strategy: Chinese propagandists prefer their points of view to appear in the local press, with local bylines. They call this "borrowing boats to reach the sea."

In this spirit, the Chinese also cooperate, both openly and discreetly, with the media outlets of other autocracies. Telesur, launched in the Chávez era, is theoretically a multinational broadcaster, but in practice its headquarters is in Caracas and its partners are Nicaragua and Cuba. Some of Telesur's content seems intended to appeal to regional, left-leaning audiences—for example, its frequent attacks on Monsanto, the giant agricultural multinational. Cherry-picked bits of foreign news also make it onto Telesur from its partners, including headlines that presumably have limited appeal in Latin America: "US-Armenia Joint Military Drills Undermine Regional Stability," for example, or "Russia Has No Expansionist Plans in Europe," both stories lifted directly from the Xinhua wire in 2023. For viewers who want related content in a different form, Iran also offers HispanTV, the Spanish-language version of PressTV, the Iranian international service, which leans more heavily into open antisemitism and Holocaust denialism. One March 2020 headline declared, "The New Coronavirus Is the Result of a Zionist Plot." Spain banned HispanTV, and Google blocked it from YouTube, but the service is easily available across Latin America, just as Al-Alam, the Arabic version of PressTV, is widely available in the Middle East.

RT—Russia Today—has a bigger profile than Telesur or PressTV and, in Africa, has closer links to China. After the channel was dropped from satellite networks following the invasion of Ukraine, RT briefly disappeared from many African countries. But after China's StarTimes satellite picked it up, RT reappeared and immediately began building offices and relationships across the continent, especially in countries run by autocrats who are eager to echo and imitate Russia's anti-Western, anti-LGBT "traditional" messages and who appreciate its lack of critical or investigative reporting. Although the Algerian government has harassed reporters from France 24, the French international channel, RT appears to be welcome now in Algiers. A South African headquarters is under construction. RT Actualidad and RT Arabic seek to reach people in Latin America and the Middle East.

The true purpose of RT, however, is not necessarily the television channel itself. RT, like PressTV, Telesur, and even China's CGTN, is rather a showcase, a production facility, and a source of video clips that can be spread by the social media network, and indeed human network, that Russians and others have constructed for that purpose. Americans got a crash course in the functioning of that network in 2016, when the Internet Research Agency, based in St. Petersburg and led at the time by the late Yevgeny Prigozhin (later more famous as a leader of a mercenary rebellion), pumped out material designed to confuse American voters. Russian-owned Facebook and Twitter accounts, pretending to be Americans, pushed out anti-immigration slogans designed to benefit Donald Trump, as well as fake "Black Lives Matter" accounts attacking Hillary Clinton from the left. They manufactured anti-Muslim hysteria in places with few Muslims, even creating a Facebook group called Secured Borders that successfully fueled an anti-refugee movement in Twin Falls, Idaho.

Since 2016, these kinds of tactics have spread. Nowadays, the Xinhua and RT offices in Africa, along with Telesur and

PressTV, all produce stories, slogans, memes, and narratives promoting the worldview of Autocracy, Inc. These are then repeated and amplified by authentic and inauthentic networks in many countries, translated into multiple languages, and reshaped for local markets. Most of the material produced is not sophisticated, but then it is also not expensive. The politicians, "experts," and media groups that use it are both real and fake. The latter sometimes hide their ownership using the same malleable company laws as kleptocratic businesses. Instead of money laundering, this is information laundering. The goal is to spread the same narratives that autocrats use at home, to connect democracy with degeneracy and chaos, to undermine democratic institutions, to smear not just activists who promote democracy but the system itself.

On February 24, 2022, as Russia swept into Ukraine, fantastical tales of biological warfare began to surge across the internet. Spokesmen for the Russian Defense and Foreign Ministries solemnly declared that secret U.S.-funded biolabs in Ukraine had been conducting experiments with bat viruses. The story was unfounded, not to say ridiculous, and it was immediately and repeatedly debunked. Nevertheless, an American Twitter account with links to the QAnon conspiracy network—@WarClandestine—began tweeting about it, racking up thousands of retweets and views. The hashtag #biolab started trending on Twitter and reached over nine million views. Even after the suspension of the account—later revealed to belong to a real person, a veteran of the Army National Guard—people continued to post screenshots. A version of the story appeared on the Infowars website, the conspiracy site created by Alex Jones, who was successfully sued for promoting conspiracy theories about the tragic school shooting at Sandy Hook. Tucker Carlson, then still a host on Fox News, played clips of a Russian general and a Chinese spokesman repeating the accusation and demanded that the Biden administration "stop lying and tell us what's going on here."

Chinese state media, backed by the Chinese government, also leaned hard into the story. A Chinese Foreign Ministry spokesman echoed his Russian colleagues, declaring that the United States controlled twenty-six biolabs in Ukraine: "Russia has found during its military operations that the U.S. uses these facilities to conduct bio-military plans." Xinhua ran multiple headlines: "U.S.-Led Biolabs Pose Potential Threats to People of Ukraine and Beyond" and "Russia Urges U.S. to Explain Purpose of Biological Labs in Ukraine." U.S. diplomats vociferously contradicted these stories. Nevertheless, the Chinese continued to spread them. So did the Asian, African, and Latin American media outlets that have content-sharing agreements with China. So did Telesur, PressTV, and the various language services of RT.

China had a clear interest in this story, since it muddied recent history and helped relieve China of the need to investigate its own hazardous biolabs, including the one in Wuhan that might have been the true source of the COVID-19 pandemic. The QAnon network, many of whose adherents promote anti-vaccination conspiracy theories, might also have been drawn to a biological-warfare conspiracy because it fits into the false QAnon narrative of American medical malpractice. Yet all three of these sources—Russian, Chinese, and extremist American—coalesce around many other themes as well. After the invasion of Ukraine, they repeated the entire range of Russian propaganda about the war, from the description of Ukrainians as "Nazis" to the claim that Ukraine is a puppet state run by the CIA. These themes then appeared several links down the food chain, in African, Asian, and Latin American media and social media.

This joint effort was successful. It helped undermine the U.S.-led effort to create international solidarity for Ukraine and enforce sanctions against Russia. In the United States, it helped undermine the Biden administration's effort to consolidate American public opinion. According to one poll, a quarter of Americans believed the biolabs conspiracy theory to be true. Russia and China, with help from some Americans and Europeans, created an international echo chamber, one in which the Venezuelans, the Iranians, and many others play supporting roles. Anyone inside this echo chamber would have heard the biolab conspiracy theory many times, always from different sources, each one repeating and building on the others to create the impression of veracity.

Even some outside the echo chamber, or those whose news outlet of choice does not have a content-sharing agreement with Xinhua, also heard the story, thanks to the other, more clandestine pathways Autocracy, Inc., uses to magnify its messages.

One of these pathways leads through organizations like

Pressenza, a website founded in Milan and relocated to Ecuador in 2014. Pressenza publishes in eight languages, describes itself as "an international news agency dedicated to news about peace and nonviolence" and did indeed publish an article on biolabs in Ukraine. But according to the U.S. State Department's Global Engagement Center, Pressenza is a Russian project, run by three Russian companies. They write articles in Moscow, translate them into Spanish, and then publish them on "native" sites in Latin America, following Chinese practice, to make them seem local. Pressenza denied these allegations; indeed, one of their journalists, Oleg Yasinsky, who claims to be of Ukrainian origin, responded by attacking "America's planetary propaganda machine" and quoting Che Guevara.

Like Pressenza, Yala News also markets itself as independent. This U.K.-registered, Arabic-language news operation provides slickly produced videos, including celebrity interviews, to its three million followers every day. In March 2022, as the biolabs allegation was being promoted by other outlets, the site posted a video that echoed one of the most sensational versions: Ukraine was planning to use migratory birds as a delivery vehicle for bioweapons, infecting the birds and then sending them into Russia to spread disease.

Yala did not invent this ludicrous tale. Russian state media published it first, followed by the Sputnik Arabic website as well as RT Arabic. Russia's UN ambassador released a long, straight-faced official statement about the "biobird scandal," warning of the "real biological danger to the people in European countries, which can result from an uncontrolled spread of bio agents from Ukraine." Some laughed: in an interview in Kyiv in April 2022, President Zelensky told me and my colleagues that the biobirds story reminded him of a *Monty Python* sketch. As a self-described "independent" publication, Yala News should have fact-checked this story, which was both mocked and widely debunked.

But Yala News is not a news organization at all. As the BBC has reported, it's an information laundromat, a site that exists to spread and propagate material produced by RT and other Russian facilities. Yala News has posted claims that the Russian massacre of Ukrainian civilians at Bucha was staged, that Zelensky appeared drunk on television, and that Ukrainian soldiers were running away from the front lines. Although the company is registered to an address in London—a mail drop shared by sixty-five thousand other companies—its "news team" is based in a suburb of Damascus, Syria. The company's CEO is a Syrian businessman based in Dubai who, when asked by the BBC, repeated his claims about "impartiality."

Why bother to cover up the company's links to Russia and Syria? Possibly the reasons were pragmatic: because the company is nominally "British," Yala News was able to evade sanctions placed on Syria and Russia and therefore able to post videos on Facebook and other platforms. But that "British" identity might also have been designed to lend the videos legitimacy, to detach them from the Russian sources that made them, and to give them extra credibility in a part of the world that is notoriously suspicious of all formal sources of news.

Yala News is not the only strange actor in this particular field. Another is African Initiative, an online news service set up in 2023 and designed specifically to spread conspiracy theories about Western public health work in Africa. The agency planned a campaign to discredit Western health philanthropy, starting with rumors about a new virus supposedly spread by mosquitoes. The idea was to smear Western doctors, clinics, and philanthropists and to build a climate of distrust around Western medicine, much as Russian efforts helped build a climate of distrust around Western vaccines during the pandemic. Again, the U.S. State Department's Global Engagement Center identified the Russian leader of the project, noted that several employees had come to the African Initiative from the Wagner Group, and located two of its offices, in Mali and Burkina Faso.

In Europe, another Russian campaign took the form of RRN—the company's name is an acronym, originally for Reliable Russian News, later changed to Reliable Recent News. Created in the wake of Russia's invasion of Ukraine, RRN, part of a bigger information-laundering operation known to investigators as *Doppelganger,* is primarily a "typosquatter": a company that registers domain names that look similar to real media domain names—Reuters.cfd instead of Reuters .com, for example—as well as websites with names that sound authentic (such as Notre Pays, or "Our Country") but are created to deceive. RRN is prolific. During its short existence, it has created more than three hundred sites in Europe, the Middle East, and Latin America. Links to these sites are then used to make Facebook, Twitter, TikTok, and other social media posts appear credible. When someone is quickly scrolling, they might not notice that a headline links to a fake Spiegel.pro website, say, rather than to the authentic German-magazine website Spiegel.de.

Doppelganger's efforts, run by a clutch of companies in Russia (including some of the same companies linked to Pressenza) have varied widely, and seem to have included a fake fact-checking website as well as fake NATO press releases, with the same fonts and design as the genuine releases, "revealing" that NATO leaders were planning to deploy Ukrainian paramilitary troops to France to quell pension protests. In November 2023, operatives whom the French government believes are linked to Doppelganger even spray-painted Stars of David around Paris, photographing them, and posting them on social media, hoping to amplify French divisions over the Gaza war.

In the autumn of 2023, some of the same team that built RRN also launched a project inside the United States. After the Biden administration proposed a large bill to fund military aid to Ukraine, Russian strategists instructed their employees to create social media posts "in the name of a resident of a suburb of a major city." According to *The Washington Post,* they were supposed to mimic an American who "doesn't support the military aid that the U.S. is giving Ukraine and considers that the money should be spent defending America's borders and not Ukraine's. He sees that Biden's policies are leading the U.S. toward collapse." In the months that followed, these kinds of posts did indeed seem to overwhelm some social media sites, as did posts about corruption in Ukraine, including one that infamously claimed, completely falsely, that President Zelensky owns two yachts.

Partly because the project was connected, again, to the idea that democracies like the United States or Ukraine are chaotic and corrupt, an idea that appeals to a part of the American Republican Party, the onslaught was successful and some of the false stories stuck. A Republican senator, Thom Tillis, told a television interviewer that during debates over aid for Ukraine, some of his colleagues, who had read the false stories, worried that "people will buy yachts with this money." Congressman Michael R. Turner, an Ohio Republican and the chairman of the House Permanent Select Committee on Intelligence, told another interviewer that "We see directly coming from Russia attempts to mask communications that are anti-Ukraine and pro-Russia messages—some of which we even hear being uttered on the House floor."

Still, the vast majority of the people who saw these ideas and repeated them had little clue as to who created them, where, or why. And this was the point: however slapdash these efforts appear to be, there is a logic behind RRN and its many sister organizations. That logic is now being studied, and copied, by other members of Autocracy, Inc.

In 2018, a typhoon stranded thousands of people at Kansai International Airport, near Osaka, Japan. Among them were some tourists from Taiwan. Normally, this story might not have had much political meaning. But a few hours into the incident, an obscure Taiwanese news website began reporting on what it said was the failure of Taiwanese diplomats to rescue their citizens. A handful of bloggers began posting on social media, too, excitedly praising Chinese officials who *had* sent buses to help their own citizens escape quickly. Some of the Taiwanese tourists had supposedly pretended to be Chinese in order to get on board. Chatter about the incident spread. Photographs and videos, allegedly from the airport, began to circulate.

The story rapidly migrated into the mainstream Taiwanese media. Journalists attacked the government: Why had Chinese diplomats moved so quickly and effectively? Why were the Taiwanese so slow and incompetent? News organizations in Taiwan described the incident as a national embarrassment, especially for a country whose leaders proclaim they have no need for support from China. Headlines declared, "To Get on the Bus, One Has to Pretend to Be Chinese" and "Taiwanese Follow China Bus." At its peak, the angry coverage and social media attacks became so overwhelming that a Taiwanese diplomat, apparently unable to bear the deluge of commentary and the shame of failure, took his life.

Subsequent investigations turned up some strange facts. Many of the people who had been posting about the incident with enthusiasm were not real; their photographs were composite images. The obscure website that first promoted the story turned out to be affiliated with the Chinese Communist Party. The videos were fake as well. Strangest of all, the Japanese government confirmed that there had been no Chinese buses, and thus no special Taiwanese failure.

Nevertheless, this semblance of failure had been pounced

upon by real Taiwanese journalists and news anchors, in particular by those who wanted to use it to attack Taiwan's ruling party, as the Chinese propagandists had surely intended. The anonymity of social media, the proliferation of "news" sites with unclear origins, and the polarization of Taiwanese politics had been manipulated in order to push one of the Chinese regime's favorite narratives: *Taiwanese democracy is weak. Chinese autocracy is strong. In an emergency, Taiwanese people want to be Chinese.*

Russian information laundering and Chinese propaganda were, until recently, rather different. The Chinese mostly stayed out of U.S. politics and the U.S. information space, except to promote Chinese achievements or Chinese narratives about Tibet, Xinjiang, and Hong Kong. Even Chinese attacks on Taiwan were carefully targeted, sometimes combining information campaigns with military threats and economic boycotts. Russian efforts, by contrast, felt more haphazard, as if a few computer hackers were throwing spaghetti at a wall, just to see which crazy story stuck.

Slowly, Chinese and Russian tactics are now converging. In 2023, following the devastating wildfire in Maui, Chinese trolls used artificial intelligence to create photographs that supposedly proved the fires were created by a secret American "weather weapon." Few picked up on these conspiracies, but they marked a notable new phase: the Chinese were experimenting, creating networks, and perhaps preparing for further disruptive operations, in the Russian style. In the spring of 2024, a group of Chinese accounts that had previously been posting pro-Chinese material in Mandarin began posting in

English, using MAGA symbols and attacking President Joe Biden. They showed fake images of Biden in prison garb, made fun of his age, and called him a satanist pedophile. One Chinese-linked account reposted an RT video repeating the lie that Biden had sent a neo-Nazi criminal to fight in Ukraine. Alex Jones's reposting of the lie on social media reached more than 400,000 people.

They are not the only ones with broad geographic ambitions. Both real and automated social media accounts geolocated to Venezuela played a small but interesting role in the 2018 Mexican presidential election, promoting the election campaign of Andrés Manuel López Obrador. Notable were two kinds of messages: those that promoted images of Mexican violence and chaos—images that might make people feel they need a strongman to restore order—and those that angrily opposed the North American Free Trade Agreement and the United States more broadly. Venezuela-based and pro-Russian trolls—one analyst called them an "entire army of zombie accounts"—were also active together in Spain, most notably at the time of the illegal 2017 independence referendum in Catalonia. Organized by Catalonia's separatist regional government without a legal basis in Spanish law, the referendum was marked by protests and scuffles with police, described on RT as "the brutal police repression against voters in the Catalan referendum." Using these kinds of headlines, alongside declarations that "Catalonia chooses its destiny between batons and rubber bullets," the trolls succeeded in reaching more people than Spanish state television.

In both the Mexican and the Catalan cases, these tiny,

inexpensive social media investments, if they helped at all, were probably judged worth the effort. After he became president, López Obrador handed over civilian enterprises to the military, undermined the independence of the judiciary, and otherwise degraded Mexican democracy. He also promoted Russian narratives about the war in Ukraine as well as Chinese narratives about the repression of the Uighurs. Mexico's relationships with the United States became more difficult, and that, surely, was part of the point.

The Catalan story had an even longer, more complicated tail. After the Spanish government annulled the illegal referendum, the former Catalan president Carles Puigdemont fled Spain. In 2019, he sent an envoy, Josep Lluís Alay, to visit Moscow. There, according to *The New York Times,* the envoy sought Russian government help in creating secret bank accounts and businesses that would finance pro-independence operations. A few months later, a strange, inorganic protest broke out in Catalonia when a protest group, allegedly with the backing of Russian intelligence, occupied a bank, shut down an airport, and blocked the main highway between France and Spain.

In neither case did the Russian and Venezuelan networks invent anything new. López Obrador is a purely Mexican figure, with a deep history in Mexican politics, not an interloper or a Russian plant. The divisions in Spain are also very old and very authentic. Both supporters and opponents of Catalan independence have been around for a long time. Antisemitism in France is equally genuine, as is antiestablishment sentiment more broadly, and that, too, is the point: autocratic information operations exaggerate the divisions and anger that are normal in politics. They pay or promote the most extreme voices, hoping to make them more extreme, and perhaps more violent; they hope to encourage people to question the state, to doubt authority, and eventually to question democracy itself.

In seeking to create chaos, these new propagandists, like their leaders, will reach for whatever ideology, whatever technology, and whatever emotions might be useful. The vehicles of disruption can be right-wing, left-wing, separatist, or nationalist, even taking the form of medical conspiracies or moral panic. Only the purpose never changes: Autocracy, Inc., hopes to rewrite the rules of the international system itself.

IV

Changing the Operating System

Before I explain how autocracies seek to bring the international system to an end, it is useful to remember how it began.

In 1946, during the early, still-optimistic days of the postwar world, the brand-new United Nations created the Commission on Human Rights. Chaired by Eleanor Roosevelt, the widow of the late president, the commission set out to write what would become the Universal Declaration of Human Rights. The original drafting committee included a Canadian legal scholar, a French jurist, a Lebanese theologian, and a Chinese philosopher. Representatives from the Soviet Union, the U.K., Chile, and Australia joined as well; at a later stage, an Indian delegate, Hansa Mehta, argued successfully that Article I of the document should declare not just that "all *men* are born free and equal" but that "all *human beings* are born free and equal." The drafters were influenced by the Christian Democracy movement, by Confucianism, by liberal legal traditions, and by the growing field of international law. Remarkably, they were united by the belief that there really could be such a thing as universal human rights, a set of principles common to all cultures and political systems.

The Soviet Union voted against the document when it was ratified in 1948, as did several Soviet satellite states. But the majority of the new UN members—Africans, Asians, and Latin Americans, as well as North Americans and Europeans—voted in favor. The document stated that "recognition of the inherent dignity and of the equal and inalienable rights of all members of the human family is the foundation of freedom, justice, and peace in the world." It also acknowledged that "disregard and contempt for human rights have resulted in barbarous acts which have outraged the conscience of mankind." Among many other principles, the declaration asserted that "everyone has the right to life, liberty, and security of person"; that no one should be subjected to "arbitrary arrest, detention or exile"; and that torture and slavery should be banned. The declaration even proclaimed that "no one shall be subjected to arbitrary interference with his privacy, family, home, or correspondence, nor to attacks upon his honor and reputation. Everyone has the right to the protection of the law against such interference or attacks."

These ideas became the basis for a score of other treaties, and for many multilateral institutions as well. The Helsinki Final Act, the treaty that recognized the inviolability of borders in Europe and formally ended World War II, states that signatories "will promote and encourage the effective exercise of civil, political, economic, social, cultural, and other rights and freedoms, all of which derive from the inherent dignity of the human person." The Charter of the Organization of American States declares that "representative democracy is an indispensable condition for the stability, peace, and development of the region."

In practice, these documents and treaties, sometimes collectively known as the rules-based order, have always described how the world *ought* to work, not how it actually works. The UN Genocide Convention did not prevent genocide in Rwanda. The Geneva Conventions did not stop the Vietnamese from torturing American prisoners of war and did not prevent Americans from torturing Iraqi prisoners of war. Signatories of the Universal Declaration of Human Rights include known violators of human rights, among them China, Cuba, Iran, and Venezuela. The UN Commission on Human Rights deteriorated into farce long ago.

Nevertheless, these documents have influenced behavior in the real world, and they still do. In the 1960s, Soviet dissidents learned to embarrass their government by pointing to human rights language in treaties the Kremlin had signed. In the first decade of the twenty-first century, Americans who mistreated Iraqi prisoners of war, in violation of the Geneva Conventions, were court-martialed, convicted, and sentenced to time in military prisons. In 2022, the UN High Commissioner for Human Rights issued a report that cataloged Chinese harassment of the Uighurs, describing the mass arrests and torture as "crimes against humanity." The Chinese reacted as might have been expected—they called the document a "patchwork of false information that serves as political tools for the U.S. and other Western countries"—

but they could not make it disappear from international media or, perhaps, from having an echo in China. In 2023, the International Criminal Court (ICC) issued arrest warrants for President Putin and Maria Lvova-Belova, Russia's commissioner for children's rights, for the crime of kidnapping and deporting thousands of Ukrainian children. Although the Russians dismissed the case as meaningless, the warrants mean the Russian president risks arrest when visiting countries that have signed the ICC treaty.

Unable to prevent these kinds of decisions, or at least not all of them, the autocracies are now leading the charge to remove that kind of language from the international arena altogether. For more than a decade, while leaders in the West have been distracted by other concerns, the Chinese have made the gradual rewriting of rules one of the central pillars of their foreign policy. At a Communist Party congress in 2017, Xi Jinping, openly declared this to be a "new era" of "great-power diplomacy with Chinese characteristics." And in this new era—a time of the "great rejuvenation of the Chinese nation"—China seeks to "take an active part in leading the reform of the global governance system." In practice, this means that China has led the charge to remove the language of human rights and democracy from international institutions. "For the CCP to attain the moral legitimacy, respect, and recognition it needs for leadership of a new world order," writes the legal scholar and China expert Andréa Worden, "it must remove the threat of Western universal human rights."

Instead of *human rights,* which are monitored by outside

organizations and independent agencies and can be measured against international standards, China wants to prioritize the *right to development,* which is something that can be defined and measured only by governments. China also relies heavily on the word *sovereignty,* which has many connotations, some of them positive. But in the context of international institutions, "sovereignty" is the word that dictators use when they want to push back against criticism of their policies, whether it comes from UN bodies, independent human rights monitors, or their own citizens. When anyone protests the Iranian regime's extrajudicial murders, the Iranian mullahs shout "sovereignty." When anyone objects to the Chinese government's repression of the people of Hong Kong, China too talks about "sovereignty." When anyone quotes the famous phrase from Article I of the UN declaration—"All human beings are born free and equal in dignity and rights"—authoritarian advocates of sovereignty dismiss such language as evidence of Western imperialism. To this general use of the term, the Russian president adds an extra twist. Sovereignty, in Putin's definition, includes the right to abuse citizens at home and to invade others abroad. This privilege is available only to a very few large nations. "There are not many countries in the world that have sovereignty," Putin said in 2017. The context made it clear that he believed Russia is sovereign but European nations are not.

To protect its sovereignty, China seeks to change other kinds of language too. Instead of "political rights" or "human rights," the Chinese want the UN and other international organizations to talk about *win-win cooperation*—by which they mean that everyone will benefit if each country maintains its own political system. They also want everyone to popularize *mutual respect*—by which they mean that no one should criticize anyone else. This vocabulary is deliberately dull and unthreatening: Who could be against "win-win cooperation" or "mutual respect"?

Nevertheless, the Chinese work extremely hard—tellingly hard—to insert such language into UN documents. If mutual respect, win-win cooperation, and sovereignty prevail, then there is no role for human rights advocates, international commissions of inquiry, or any public criticism of Chinese policy in Tibet, Hong Kong, or Xinjiang at all. The UN's already limited ability to investigate UN member states will be curtailed further.

While China seeks to change the way diplomats and bureaucrats talk inside the UN, Russia has mostly focused its efforts on changing the popular conversation around the world. If win-win sounds nice, then *multipolarity,* the word that Russian information networks now prefer, could have an even greater appeal. A multipolar world is meant to be fair and equitable, unlike the America-centric world, or the American hegemony they are trying to abolish. The word is especially useful because it is often used, neutrally, to express the idea that there are more nations with international clout than there were in the past, which is merely an accurate observation. "We are moving towards a multipolar world," said the UN secretary-general, António Guterres, in 2023.

This idea is hardly novel: the journalist Fareed Zakaria published a book describing the "rise of the rest," the growing power of new global powers, more than fifteen years ago.

As part of a more recent Russian narrative about the end of universal values, the word has also acquired a vaguely Marxist echo, as if previously repressed countries were removing their oppressors. In service of this idea, Russia, itself a colonial power, paints itself as a leader of former colonies, calling for what the analyst Ivan Klyszcz describes as messianic multipolarity, a battle against the West's imposition of "decadent," "globalist" values. In September 2022, when the Russian president held a ceremony to mark his illegal annexation of southern and eastern Ukraine, he did not speak of the people he had tortured or held in concentration camps, but instead claimed he was protecting Russia from the "satanic" West and "perversions that lead to degradation and extinction." A few months later, Putin told a gathering in Moscow, "We are now fighting for the freedom of not only Russia, but the whole world. . . . We openly say that the dictatorship of one hegemon—we see it, everyone sees it now—is decrepit. It has gone, as they say, into disarray and is simply dangerous for those around us."

The irony of course is that Russia is a genuine danger for everyone around Russia, which is why most of Russia's neighbors, including now Sweden and Finland, are rearming and preparing to fight against Russian colonial occupation. The anticolonial tone creates ironies elsewhere too. Since 2021, Russian mercenaries from the Wagner Group have helped keep a military dictatorship in power in Mali, where they have been accused of carrying out summary executions, committing atrocities against civilians, and looting property. In Mali, as in Ukraine, multipolarity means that brutal white Russian thugs now play a large role in public life. And yet Mali Actu, a pro-Russian website in Mali, solemnly explains to its readers that "in a world that is more and more multipolar, Africa will play a more and more important role."

However ironic or sinister, *multipolarity* is now the basis for a whole campaign, systematically spread on RT in English, French, Spanish, and Arabic, repeated by information-laundering sites such as Yala News, stated again and again by a thousand other cutouts, think tanks, and paid and unpaid pro-Russian journalists, as well as other spokesmen for Autocracy, Inc. Xinhua celebrated the African Union's membership in the G20—the Group of 20 conference of the world's largest economies—as evidence of "the aggressive emergence of the multipolar world." The China Global Television Network, in a web article illustrated with a photograph of the Syrian dictator, Bashir al-Assad—who massacres his own people—informs its viewers that "China's diplomacy injects vitality into the multipolar world." President Maduro of Venezuela has spoken of "the multipolar, pluricentric world that we yearn for, and that we are united for, with our flags of struggle with all of the peoples of the world." When he visited China, he tweeted that his trip would "strengthen ties of cooperation and the construction of a new global geopolitics." North Korea has expressed its desire to cooperate with Russia "to establish a 'new multi-polarized international order.'" When the president of Iran, Ebrahim Raisi, in 2023 visited the three most important Latin American autocracies, Venezuela, Cuba, and Nicaragua, he said that the purpose of his trip was to "stand against imperialism and unilateralism," by which he meant he wanted to solidify their opposition to democracy and universal rights.

Slowly, the countries leading the assault on the language of rights, human dignity, and the rule of law are creating institutions of their own. Members of the Shanghai Cooperation Organization—China, India, Kazakhstan, Kyrgyzstan, Russia, Pakistan, Tajikistan, Uzbekistan (Afghanistan, Belarus, Iran, and Mongolia have observer status)—all agree to recognize one another's "sovereignty," not to criticize one another's autocratic behavior, and not to intervene in one another's internal politics. The group of countries known as BRICS (the acronym stands for Brazil, Russia, India, China, and South Africa, and was originally a term coined by a Goldman Sachs economist to describe emerging-market business opportunities) is also transforming itself into an alternative international institution, with regular meetings and new members. In January 2024, Iran, Saudi Arabia, Egypt, the U.A.E., and Ethiopia were welcomed into the group, the better to give it the flavor of a new, Moscow- and Beijing-oriented world order.

Groups like BRICS and the Shanghai Cooperation Organization are sometimes dismissed as more talk than substance—an annual excuse for a photo op. But they represent something real. Though not every leader who joins these meetings is an autocrat—the BRICS group in particular does not have a unified political position—many want to use these institutions to help spread the same kind of unfettered power they enjoy at home around the world. If the old system was designed to inculcate the "rule of law," these new institutions are meant to promote "rule by law"—the belief that "law" is whatever the current autocrat or ruling party leader says it is, whether inside Iran, Cuba, or anywhere else in the world. And just as the old system of universal rights had implications for the real behavior of nations, this new one does too.

When reading about "international law" or "human rights," people from the democratic world may still feel a sense of distance, a lack of direct threat. Surely their own political systems will protect anyone who lives in them from the lawlessness that prevails in Russia or Cuba; surely there are some rules and regulations that the international community will always share—the laws of the sea, for example, or the norms governing the conduct of air traffic controllers. In 2021, the dictator of Belarus, Alexander Lukashenko, shattered that basic assumption in a stunt with no exact precedent, asking Belarusian aviation authorities to divert a plane owned by Ryanair, an Irish company, that was crossing through Belarusian airspace on its way from Athens, Greece, to Vilnius, Lithuania, from one part of the European Union to another. Belarusian air traffic control falsely told the pilots that the plane had a bomb on board. According to Belarusian state media, the plane was then "escorted" to Minsk, the capital of Belarus, by a MiG fighter jet.

In reality, there was no bomb, the threat was fake, and

Minsk was not even the closest airport. After the plane landed, nobody rushed to get the passengers to safety. The true purpose of the stunt became clear after two passengers were removed: Roman Protasevich, a Belarusian opposition blogger and journalist, and his girlfriend, Sofia Sapega. Protasevich was one of the original editors of Nexta, a Telegram blogging channel that became one of the most important sources of public information during the enormous anti-regime demonstrations that took place in Minsk in 2020. He had fled the country and had been living in exile ever since. In absentia, the Belarusian state had declared him a "terrorist," and as soon as the plane started its descent, he knew that he was the target. "I am facing the death penalty," he told one of the other passengers. In the end, the state did not kill him, but he was subjected to brutal interrogations, isolation, and torture, just like so many other political prisoners in Belarus. He finally made a grotesque televised confession, renounced his friends, and abandoned Sapega in order to save his life.

That Lukashenko was willing to falsely detain and possibly endanger a European-owned, European-registered airplane carrying mostly European citizens from one European nation to another meant both that he was prepared for a total break with Europe and that he was completely confident of economic and political support from the autocratic world. His confidence was well placed. Although the hijacking was followed by the usual Western protests, and although the Belarusian national airline was banned from European airspace, Lukashenko paid no higher price. There was no international institution with the clout to punish him or to free

Protasevich. The Belarusian dictator was protected by "sovereignty" and by his friends. In the immediate wake of the incident, the head of RT tweeted that the hijacking made her "envy" Belarus. Lukashenko, she wrote, "performed beautifully." Another senior Russian official called the hijacking "feasible and necessary."

Although this was probably the first time that an autocratic regime abused air-traffic-control procedures to kidnap a dissident, it was hardly the first time that autocracies had reached beyond their borders to harass, arrest, or kill their own citizens. The human rights organization Freedom House calls this practice "transnational repression" and has compiled more than six hundred examples. Sometimes, intelligence agents or assassins commit these crimes. Employees of the GRU, Russian military intelligence, have used radioactive poisons and nerve agents against enemies of the Kremlin in London and Salisbury, England, where their target survived but they accidentally murdered a British woman. Another assassin, sent by the Russian state, murdered a former Chechen fighter in the center of Berlin. Russian critics and business executives have met mysterious deaths by falling down flights of stairs or out of windows in India, the south of France, and Washington, D.C. Over more than four decades, the Islamic Republic of Iran has also killed or tried to kill Iranian exiles in Europe—Denmark, France, Germany, the Netherlands, Sweden, the U.K.—as well as the Middle East, Latin America, and the United States, with the numbers rising sharply over the past decade. In January 2023, the U.S. government indicted three members of a criminal gang—

originally from Azerbaijan, Russia, and Georgia—for plotting on behalf of the Iranian government to murder Masih Alinejad, an outspoken critic of the Iranian regime and a U.S. citizen, at her home in Brooklyn.

Sometimes, autocracies support one another in these kinds of efforts, helping give them a quasi-legal sheen. Members of the Shanghai Cooperation Organization have agreed to jointly fight terrorism, separatism, and extremism, for example, with each state effectively agreeing to recognize the others' definitions of those words. In practice that means that if China says one of its exiled citizens is a criminal, then Russia, Kazakhstan, or any of the other members will have that person deported back to China. But these definitions are beginning to apply in more countries, including some hybrid democracies that feel pressure from Russia and China. Thailand, which is not a member of the Shanghai Cooperation Organization, has detained Russian dissidents and deported members of the Uighur minority back to China. Turkey, a country that until recently supported the Uighurs out of a sense of kinship—they are Muslim and speak a Turkic language—has begun to arrest and deport Uighurs too. "When you stand against China," one Uighur dissident has said, "you are a threat wherever you are."

China also keeps close track of the Chinese diaspora, wherever its members are. Chinese democracy activists living in the United States and Canada have been visited by Chinese agents who try to persuade them, or blackmail them, to return home. Some are threatened over the telephone or online. Ciping Huang, the executive director of the Wei Jingsheng Foundation, named after one of China's most famous democracy activists, told me that the group's offices in the Washington, D.C., area have been broken into more than a dozen times over the past decade. Old computers have disappeared, phone lines have been cut, and mail has been thrown in the toilet, presumably just to let the activists know that someone was there. In 2023, the FBI arrested two people for operating an illegal Chinese "police station" in New York City, a set of offices used by Chinese security officers to monitor Chinese citizens and dissidents. The Dutch government says it has uncovered two illegal Chinese police stations in the Netherlands as well, and there are accounts and rumors of others.

Smaller autocracies have followed suit. In February 2024, four men passing themselves off as Chilean police detectives abducted and murdered Ronald Ojeda, an exiled former Venezuelan military officer from his home in Santiago, Chile—he was found dismembered and encased under five feet of concrete nine days later. The Rwandan government has harassed, assaulted, or murdered dissident exiles in at least six countries, including Belgium, where a former politician was found floating in a canal, and South Africa, where a former military leader was shot in the stomach. Paul Rusesabagina, who sheltered more than a thousand people from the 1994 Rwandan genocide, and whose story became the subject of *Hotel Rwanda,* an Oscar-nominated movie, emigrated from his country after he clashed with the Rwandan president, Paul Kagame. Although he was living in the United States, in 2020 he was conned into boarding a private plane in

Dubai and flown back to Kigali, where he was immediately imprisoned. Even India, a hybrid democracy, has begun to track political opponents around the world. In 2023, Indian agents are alleged to have murdered Hardeep Singh Nijjar, a Sikh community leader in Canada, and to have plotted the murder of another in the United States.

The primary purpose of these attacks is, of course, the elimination, intimidation, or neutralization of political exiles. Even from a distance an eloquent critic can nowadays have an impact, whether through a YouTube channel, through a WhatsApp group, or just because he remains true to his beliefs, despite the regime's efforts, and because he becomes a symbol of hope. Transnational repression also degrades the rule of law in the countries where the crimes take place. Slowly, the police in the target country become accustomed to the violence; after all, it mostly affects foreigners. The government officials who have been sympathetic to the exiles or their causes also become numb or uninterested in the harassment; after all, they have other things to do. The stories are not covered in the local press, or if so, only sporadically. The idea that China, Rwanda, or Iran *simply can't be stopped*—this is just their nature, this is just the way they are—becomes part of the culture. Democracies simply come to accept lawlessness, even within their own borders. Which is not surprising, since they are coming to accept violence on a much larger scale too.

—

In September 2018, the United Nations stepped in to de-escalate the situation in Idlib, the northwest region of Syria. "De-escalation" is a euphemism: it's what happens when diplomats can't stop a war but are trying to save people's lives anyway. Syria was an active war zone, convulsed by violence since 2011. In that year the Syrian dictator had turned against peaceful demonstrators who were hoping to end his brutal regime. Assad might well have lost the civil war that followed, had the Iranian government not sent fighters, advisers, intelligence, and weapons and had the Russian military, in 2015, not entered the conflict on the side of the Syrian regime. If the dictators of Venezuela, Zimbabwe, and Belarus have been propped up by propaganda, surveillance technology, and economic aid from the autocratic world, Assad was saved in a less subtle manner, by Russian and Iranian bullets.

The two armies had different motives. Iran needed access to Syrian territory because Iran sends weapons and fighters to Iranian proxies nearby, Hezbollah in Lebanon, Hamas and other small groups in Palestine, Iraq, and Syria itself. Syria's hostility to Israel suited the Iranians too. Even if he wasn't completely aligned with the Islamic Republic's religious war, Assad was an extra lever, an extra threat, and an extra ally in the region.

Putin's logic was surely broader. He probably intervened because the Arab Spring that preceded the Syrian uprising scared him, because it looked too much like the "color revolution" he fears in Russia, and because he wanted to show Russians that political mobilization and political protest will end in bloody tragedy. He also wanted to preserve Russia's long-standing ties to Syria and prove that he could compete as an equal with the United States in the Middle East. Two years earlier, President Barack Obama had refused to intervene after the Syrian government used chemical weapons—weapons built with Iranian assistance—even after promising to do so. Putin spotted the opportunity to outflank Obama and to demonstrate what he really meant by multipolarity and a new world order. Over the course of the next several years, Russian, Syrian, and Iranian troops jointly went out of their way to break every possible norm, every element of international law that they possibly could.

One of those tests took place in Idlib. At that time, the province was one of the few remaining territories controlled by the Syrian opposition. As a part of the "de-escalation," the UN asked all participants in the conflict to avoid hitting hospitals and medical facilities. The UN even provided the Russian government the exact coordinates of hospitals and medical facilities in Idlib, in order to protect those buildings. But instead of protecting them, the Russians and Syrian pilots *used the UN coordinates to guide missiles to the hospitals.* After a series of direct hits, medical teams on the ground stopped sharing information with the UN.

That jaw-dropping fact should have alarmed the world. "Today in Syria, the abnormal is now normal. The unacceptable is accepted," said Joanne Liu, the president of Doctors Without Borders, the medical charity. "The normalization of such attacks is intolerable." Nevertheless, normalization followed. No special measures were taken; in practice, Europe and North America accepted Russian targeting of hospitals. In practice, the world also accepted a separate Syrian air force attack on a UN convoy that was described, in a UN report, as "meticulously planned and ruthlessly carried out . . . to purposefully hinder the delivery of humanitarian aid and target aid workers." The scale of the violence in Syria helped lay the groundwork for the rise of ISIS, the fanatical cult; for the brutal Hamas attack in Israel on October 7, 2023; for Hamas's use of hospitals as shelters in Gaza; and for Israeli strikes on hospitals and other civilian objects in Gaza too. When the United Nations Relief and Works Agency in Palestine was found to be harboring Hamas fighters, no one was surprised: the UN, unable to stop a member of the Security Council from violating its rules, was no longer capable of preventing employees of its own agencies from engaging in lawless violence either.

The Syrian civil war also created another kind of precedent. For the first time, one side in a conflict deliberately made international institutions and humanitarian aid workers a central focus of their war propaganda. The fire hose of falsehoods, Kremlin-backed writers disguised as journalists, and thousands of social media accounts familiar from other campaigns were repeatedly used to discredit the Organisation for the Prohibition of Chemical Weapons, which was investigating the Syrian use of sarin gas and other chemicals, in order to claim that film or evidence of those attacks was fake or staged.

The same network, enhanced by far-left and alt-right British and American academics, pundits, trolls, and bloggers, also successfully smeared the White Helmets, a team of thirty-three hundred volunteer first responders, Syrian civilians who helped tens of thousands of Syrians recover from bombing campaigns, literally pulling people from the rubble. The White Helmets, more formally known as Syria Civil Defence, also documented Syrian government attacks with photographs, video, and personal testimony. Following the Syrian government's use of sarin gas in 2017, a White Helmet volunteer testified that he'd seen people "fainting completely unconscious . . . cases of trembling and convulsions, foam coming out of the respiratory tract and mouth." People believed him because the White Helmets were ordinary people who helped other ordinary people, because their work created trust. The Russians knew this, which is why they sought to undermine that trust, linking the White Helmets alternately to George Soros and al-Qaeda, claiming that their rescue operations were "staged," smearing their donors as supporters of terrorism as well.

The Russian campaign against the White Helmets reached millions of people, not least because Russian propagandists learned to game algorithms even before social media companies understood what had happened. In April 2018, I typed "White Helmets" into a YouTube search engine and found that seven of the first ten results were links to videos produced by RT. They sowed doubt about whether chemical weapons had ever been used at all, and even if they had, they argued that the Syrian opposition, not the government, was responsible. The sheer quantity of contradictory material was also meant, again, to convince people that the truth was impossible to know. But something else was at stake as well. The White Helmets created feelings of solidarity, humanity, and hope. To win the war, Russia and Iran needed ordinary Syrians to feel despair and apathy, and the rest of the world to feel helpless. They succeeded.

Over time, Europeans stopped talking about the war. Instead, they focused their attention on an unprecedented wave of Syrian refugees, large enough to destabilize the Continent's politics and to shape a series of European elections, from the Polish election in 2015 to the British Brexit referendum in 2016, right up to the European parliamentary elections of 2024. Concerns about the numbers of migrants were amplified by far-right trolling operations and by Russian campaigns, as well as by several prominent terrorist attacks from groups with roots or financing in the autocratic world. The Arab world accepted the violence in Syria too. Having expelled Assad for shooting at unarmed demonstrators in 2011, the Arab League finally welcomed him back in 2023. With a straight face, the dictator whose regime was saved by Russia and Iran accepted his readmission with a call for "non-intervention." "It is important to leave internal affairs to the country's people as they are best able to manage their own affairs," he said.

Xi Jinping also endorsed the outcome of the Syrian war, even journeying to Iran, in 2016, to announce a new partnership with the regime that had helped destroy Syria. "We decided to turn our mutual relations into . . . strategic relations," Xi declared. Iran, meanwhile, created a new foreign policy slogan—"Turning East"—and signed an agreement giving China access to discounted Iranian oil as well as to the Iranian petrochemical, infrastructure, telecommunications, and banking markets. These deals weakened the sanctions that the Trump administration placed on Iran, which was part of the point.

Finally, the Syrian war set the precedent for new forms of military engagement. In addition to the regular Russian military forces and the Iranian advisers, a host of proxies and mercenaries, fighters with links to recognized states but with their own sources of funding (and, sometimes, their own motives), dominated parts of the battlefield. First among these proxies is the Wagner Group, the corporate name for several mercenary groups formed to fight in eastern Ukraine in 2014, then sent to Libya and Syria soon afterward. From the start, Wagner was funded and supplied by the Russian state, both directly and through government contracts arranged with Yevgeny Prigozhin, Wagner's de facto CEO. Because Wagner advertised itself as "private," the Russian state could distance itself from its activities and from the people involved. If they died in combat, they were not "Russian army soldiers," and the state did not have to acknowledge them. Unlike regular soldiers, Wagner commanders could also do business deals in the places where they operated, arranging mining concessions or the export of minerals and other goods, both for personal profit and to pay for their equipment and ammunition.

Iranian proxies play a similar role. Hezbollah and Hamas, like the Houthis in Yemen and many smaller groups, are usually described as terrorist organizations rather than mercenary groups, but some of their operating methods are similar. Just as the states of Autocracy, Inc., share no ideology, the Iranian proxies share no ideology with Wagner or, sometimes, even with one another. They do resemble their Russian counterparts in other ways. Like Wagner, Iranian-backed groups recruit professional soldiers, maintain extensive business interests, and conduct propaganda campaigns, all with various degrees of Iranian backing. Hezbollah runs a political party in Lebanon and produces television series and programs. Hamas, before attacking Israel in October 2023, ran Gaza as its own fiefdom, a miniature autocratic state. The Houthis, trained by Hezbollah, control a region of Yemen, but also see themselves as players in a global conflict, with Israel and the United States as their main opponents. They all have a similar contempt for international rules of any kind, a radicalism that is sometimes strong enough to overcome even Shiite-Sunni or other religious divisions.

Similar military-financial packages, including weapons, off-the-books soldiers, propagandists, and advisers, are now being offered to others. Wagner mercenaries arrived in Mali in 2021, invited by a military regime, following a coup, to replace French and other forces who had been helping fight off an Islamic insurgency. Even before the coup, pro-Russian media, pro-Russian organizations, and Russian-style disinformation campaigns against France and the UN appeared in Mali; since the coup, Russians have gained access to three Malian gold mines, among other assets.

A parallel story unfolded in the Central African Republic after the president of that country invited Wagner troops to help him fight off an insurgency as well. Now Wagner mercenaries guard the president and brutally repress his enemies. They run a radio station that produces Russian and government propaganda and rails against "modern practices of neo-colonialism." In March 2022, a Russian diplomat instructed the Central African Republic's top court to alter the constitution so that the country's pro-Russian president could stay in power beyond his two-term limit. When the court's top judge objected, he was removed. In return for these services, the Russians have obtained mining licenses, sometimes by intimidating the previous owners, as well as the right to export diamonds, gold, and timber without paying tax.

Like the founders of so many other successful start-ups, the original investors in Wagner's African operation appear to be contemplating the creation of a franchise. A team from Britain's Royal United Services Institute has described the current Russian offer to sitting dictators and would-be dictators as a "regime survival package." This bundle of aid can include personal protection for the dictator; violent assaults on his political enemies; help in fighting an insurgency; broadcast or social media campaigns that echo the themes of multipolarity and anticolonialism; kleptocratic contacts that help the elite hide money (and possibly benefit the Russians as well). By accepting this package, the local dictator will also be cut off from democratic allies, either because the violence and repression needed to maintain power make him too unpalatable or because his new Russian allies insist he cut ties with old American and European friends.

Maybe, in the future, other autocracies will contribute to these kinds of packages as well. Chinese investment might be made available to the right kind of regime, to help undermine sanctions. Iran could tailor an Islamic insurgency to help topple a wobbling democratic government. Expertise in the international narcotics trade could be provided by the Venezuelans; the Zimbabweans could help with gold smuggling. If all that sounds far-fetched, it shouldn't. A world in which autocracies work together to stay in power, work together to promote their system, and work together to damage democracies is not some distant dystopia. That world is the one we are living in right now.

V

Smearing the Democrats

"IN RECENT YEARS various dictatorships—of both internal and external origin—have collapsed or stumbled when confronted by defiant, mobilized people."

Those are the opening words of *From Dictatorship to Democracy,* an iconic pamphlet composed by Gene Sharp, an American academic. Sharp emerged from the world of pacifism, civil rights, and antiwar activism in the 1950s to become, by the 1990s, an advocate of nonviolent revolution. A student of Gandhi, King, and Thoreau, Sharp believed that dictatorships survive not because of the unusual powers or personalities of dictators but because most people who live under their rule are apathetic or afraid. He believed that if they overcame their apathy and fear, and that if they refused to acquiesce to the dictator's demands, then the dictator would no longer be able to rule.

Sharp was a pragmatist, not a dreamer. He opposed the use of violence not merely on moral grounds but because it is an ineffective means of fighting a dictatorship: "By placing confidence in violent means, one has chosen the very type of struggle with which the oppressors nearly always have superiority." Democratic activists who use force against an autocratic regime usually lose, he argued. They have less firepower and fewer resources than the state. They are rarely able to create armies. Sharp argued that social movements should instead begin by "identifying the Achilles' heel" of the dictator, the areas in which he is weak or vulnerable. They should systematically consolidate the opposition, fight fear and apathy, persuade people to demonstrate their resistance to the regime, and rob the regime's leaders of their legitimacy. The goal is to take power, but to do so peacefully.

From Dictatorship to Democracy was originally published in Bangkok, in 1994, as a primer for Burmese democracy activists. But Sharp's suggestions were applicable almost anywhere, and eventually they were reprinted almost everywhere, in many languages, legally and illegally. The most frequently copied part of the pamphlet was its appendix, which contains a list of 198 nonviolent, anti-authoritarian tactics. These include speeches, letters, declarations, and mass petitions; protest songs and plays; skywriting and "methods of economic noncooperation"; and peasant and prisoners' strikes, slowdown strikes, quick "lightning" strikes, "sick-ins," and more than a dozen other kinds of strikes. Sharp also listed "physical interventions," including sit-ins, stand-ins, ride-ins, wade-ins, pray-ins, and "nonviolent occupation" of public spaces "as well as 'action by holders of financial resources,' including the withdrawal of bank deposits, refusal to pay fees, refusal to pay debts or interest, and severance of funds and credit." And so on.

In time, the list took on a life of its own. Without Sharp's name or any other attribution, his list was circulating in Cairo, in Arabic, at the time of the Tahrir Square uprising in 2011. He was then eighty-three years old, but that might also have been the moment when Sharp's fame reached its peak. In the wake of the Arab Spring, he was profiled twice by *The New York Times.* He was cited as an influence in Serbia, Syria, Venezuela, Belarus, and Iran. He was attacked for his alleged (in fact, nonexistent) links to the CIA.

Plenty of people who led mass demonstrations around that time denied that he had influenced them, and in a strict sense that was probably true. Protesters often adopted these kinds of tactics not because of anything Sharp had done or said but because they had already been used elsewhere, and because they were perceived to be effective. More to the point, they *were* effective. Activists around the world looked at what had happened in the Philippines in 1986, or in East Germany in 1989, and they wanted the same.

Most of these movements learned far more from one another than they did from Gene Sharp, and they certainly had nothing to do with "foreign agents" or the CIA. Back in 1980, long before Sharp published his pamphlet, Solidarity—Poland's independent, anticommunist, and at the time illegal trade union movement—created a logo that was recognizable across the country and around the world: the Polish word *solidarność,* written in squiggly letters, red on a white background, evoking the Polish flag. It was featured on posters, worn on lapels, printed in underground journals, and understood everywhere as a sign of opposition. Knowing the history of this symbol, Otpor (the word means "resistance"), a Serbian youth movement created in 1998 to oppose Slobodan Milosevic, created a logo too: a black-and-white drawing of a fist within a circle and the word *Otpor,* followed by an exclamation point. The same idea, in a different form, was adopted by the Georgian democracy activists who used a red rose as their symbol, and by the protesters who wore orange to protest stolen elections in 2004 in Ukraine.

Sharp called these tactics "symbolic acts" and believed they served a purpose that would have been familiar to an older philosopher of civic opposition, the playwright Václav Havel. In a 1978 essay, "The Power of the Powerless," Havel asked his readers to imagine that a greengrocer, an ordinary citizen in what was then communist Czechoslovakia, "places in his window, among the onions and carrots, the slogan: 'Workers of the world, unite!' " Havel then asked, why does he do it?

The greengrocer is probably not genuinely enthusiastic about the international working class, Havel wrote, nor does he care whether its members unite. Rather, he has placed the sign in the window to demonstrate his symbolic loyalty to the regime, knowing that if he does not do so, there could be trouble. He won't go to prison or lose his job. But "he could be reproached for not having the proper decoration in his window; someone might even accuse him of disloyalty." He does it, Havel writes, "because these things must be done if one is to get along in life."

The sign has a second purpose: it helps the greengrocer conceal his obedience to the state from himself. He can hide his low motives—his desire to get on in life—beneath a higher motive: the "unity of the workers of the world." But as soon as someone walks into this imaginary shop wearing a *solidarność* badge (in Warsaw in 1980) or an *Otpor* T-shirt (in Belgrade in 1998) or carrying a rose (in Tbilisi in 2003) or wearing an orange jacket (in Kyiv in 2004–5), the greengrocer's ideology is exposed. He confronts people who have decided to say what they think and to advertise what they believe, despite the regime. To use Havel's language, these are people who want to "live in truth."

These small, symbolic acts of bravery force the greengrocer to face the fact that he has been living a lie. He may or may not change his behavior as a result. Perhaps he will respond by deciding to become a true partisan of the regime. But at least he has now made a conscious choice. Havel believed that if everyone were forced to choose, and if everybody were forced to confront propaganda with reality, then sooner or later the falsehoods promulgated by the regime would be exposed.

The display of symbols—badges, flowers, logos, colors—to force people to take sides is only one of many tactics that spread from one democratic movement to another in the last decades of the twentieth century and the first decades of the twenty-first from the Philippines, South Korea, and Taiwan to the post-Soviet world to the Middle East—the Cedar Revolution in Lebanon, the Green Movement in Iran, the Arab Spring—and beyond. The deliberate creation of links between different social groups and social classes is another such tactic. The anticommunist Hungarian revolution of 1956 was made possible because factory workers, and eventually soldiers and police, joined Budapest intellectuals in protest. The Solidarity movement in Poland in 1980–81 created explicit relationships between shipyard workers in Gdańsk, led by the electrician Lech Wałęsa, and the union's "advisers," who were journalists, lawyers, and historians from Warsaw.

Creating bonds between different classes and across different geographies is not just a matter of activism. It also requires an idea or a set of ideas large enough to overcome class and social divisions. For some, universal principles of freedom and free speech matter most. Others are driven by the experience of injustice or state violence. In many cases, the gap between the stated principles of the constitution and the reality offered by the regime is enough to inspire calls for change. In Iran, reports of a stolen election in 2009 sparked a mass protest movement. In 2011, when it became clear that Vladimir Putin was planning to return to power—having already served the constitutional limit of two terms—demonstrations against fraudulent and unconstitutional elections were staged over many months in Moscow and St. Petersburg.

In 2016, in Venezuela, after the opposition won a majority in parliament but was prevented from legislating, millions of people participated in more than a thousand separate protests. In 2020, following a blatantly stolen election, Belarusians organized protests for the first time in their history. They wore red and white, the colors of the alternative (and illegal) Belarusian flag, as they literally danced and sang in the streets; policemen and soldiers joined them, some ripping off insignia and burning them in public.

Sometimes the fame or notoriety of the leader can unify a movement. Aung San Suu Kyi, the daughter of a previous independence leader who had spent years under house arrest, became the obvious focal point for the first, not entirely successful democratic revolution in Myanmar. But the leader can also be apolitical, someone perceived as an outsider who is above the fray and not seeking personal power: Sviatlana Tsikhanouskaya, a housewife whose husband was imprisoned for political activism, became first the presidential candidate and then the leader of the Belarus protests of 2020 precisely because she was seen as someone who cared about ordinary people like herself.

In more recent years, activists have modernized, adopting tactics that neither Sharp nor Havel could have imagined. Nobody needs to smuggle *From Dictatorship to Democracy* or "The Power of the Powerless" over a border in an era of encrypted messaging services. VPNs—virtual private networks—and other tools can be used to access blocked information on the internet; messages can spread on social media, on the dark web, through custom-made apps. Funding a movement is easier when activists can transfer money to one another using bitcoin, avoiding both the banking system and the secret police.

In the past decade, no political group took all these lessons on board with greater skill and thoughtfulness than the Hong Kong democracy movement, which was demanding that the Chinese regime live up to its own promises. In 1997, when the British handed the territory back to China after 156 years of colonial rule, the Chinese leadership promised that the economic and political freedoms Hong Kong enjoyed would be preserved. The promise was encapsulated in the slogan "one country, two systems." Over the next two decades, China increased its overt and subtle pressure on Hong Kong. In 2014, Beijing changed the Hong Kong electoral system to allow the Communist Party to screen candidates for the Hong Kong chief executive's role in advance. Recognizing this "reform" as the beginning of an assault on Hong Kong's democracy, and even an attempt to alter its identity, protesters staged a series of sit-ins. They took over several public spaces in Hong Kong and set up camp on them, naming their movement Occupy Central. They carried umbrellas to protect themselves from tear gas and pepper spray—hence another name, the Umbrella Movement. The protest did not achieve its aims, not least because it proved impossible to occupy public spaces over a long period of time, but the protesters learned lessons, studied their mistakes, and prepared for what came next.

In 2019, provoked by a law that would have required Hong Kong criminals to be extradited to China—thereby extending Chinese legal jurisdiction over Hong Kong—a wide range of activists again organized a new round of demonstrations. This time, there was no single leader and no organizing committees that could be penetrated or arrested. Instead of staging long occupations of the city center, the protesters surprised the police by appearing on different days in different places. They used apps to track police movements, painted their faces to fool video surveillance cameras, and called upon one another to "be like water"—to stay flexible, to change tactics hour by hour if need be.

They also learned from the experiences of others. From protests staged in the Baltic states in 1989, they borrowed the idea of creating a mass human chain. From the Ukrainian protests of 2014, they learned to wear helmets and gas masks if they expected clashes with police. They maintained anonymity using codes and pseudonyms. They used banners and posters to reach the public in a society where much of the internet is controlled by the state. They deployed "noncooperation" tactics to disrupt everyday life. They crowdfunded advertisements in the international press. They used Sharp's tactics, and many more.

Their goal was not just to change government policy, but to change society, to raise awareness, to teach people how to resist an autocratic and increasingly brutal regime—and they did. The protesters of Hong Kong put up the longest and toughest fight anyone has conducted against Chinese authoritarianism. Their efforts were more sustained and systematic than the Tiananmen Square protests of 1989, cleverer and more flexible than their own Umbrella Movement of a few years earlier. The protests transcended barriers of social class and involved millions of people, rich and poor.

But although they won battle after battle, they lost the war. As of this writing, all the Hong Kong protest leaders are in jail or in exile. Many of those who remain in Hong Kong are working in menial jobs.

They did everything right. But they were defeated because the Chinese authorities had also been studying the kinds of tactics proposed by Sharp and Havel. They had thought hard about how to mock and undermine symbolic acts; how to smear and discredit charismatic leaders; how to use social media to spread false rumors and conspiracy theories; how to isolate and alienate people; how to break links between different social groups and social classes; how to eliminate influential exiles; and above all, how to turn the language of human rights, freedom, and democracy into evidence of treason and betrayal. The rest of Autocracy, Inc., learned these lessons too.

In April 2016, Evan Mawarire, a Pentecostal pastor in Zimbabwe, sat down in his office, draped the national flag around his neck, peered into the camera on his telephone, and pressed Record. Over the next several minutes, Mawarire made a brief, unrehearsed speech of exceptional power, describing Zimbabwe's flag and the meaning of its colors, one by one:

> They tell me that the green is for the vegetation and the crops. . . . I don't see any crops in my country.
>
> The yellow is for all the minerals, gold, diamonds, platinum, chrome. . . . I don't know how much of it is left, I don't know who they sold it to and how much they got for it.
>
> The red, they say it's for the blood, the blood that was shed to secure freedom for me and I'm so thankful

> for that. I just don't know that if they were here—they that shed the blood—and saw the way this country is, would they demand their blood be brought back?
>
> The black is for the majority, people like me. Yet for some reason I don't feel like I am a part of it.

Years later, Mawarire told me that he had made that video out of desperation. He had a good education, and he had children he hoped to educate too. He had lived in the U.K. for several years, but had returned to Zimbabwe in 2008, the moment when, briefly, change seemed possible. But instead of changing, Zimbabwe slid deeper into political and economic crisis. Inflation reduced the pensions of Mawarire's elderly parents to nothing. Mawarire himself could barely make ends meet. His desperation impelled him to make the video.

He had no special contacts with foreigners, no links to Europeans or Americans who promote democracy, and no background in politics. He was a youth pastor, not a politician or a social media influencer. But although he had not led any kind of movement before, his words came from the heart. The collapse of the Zimbabwean economy, he told me, had "finally knocked on my own door, and the reality was now present in the form of an empty dinner table."

His video went viral, and so did his hashtag, #ThisFlag. Mawarire became a celebrity. People came up to him on the street and thanked him, he told me. "You have said what I have felt for so many years," they would tell him. Or else, "You are saying what I have felt for a long time but have not known how to channel." At first, he thought, "It'll go away, it'll blow over, the excitement will die down, and that's it, nothing will come out of it." Instead, the excitement kept building. For a brief, heady moment, #ThisFlag became a nationwide phenomenon, a unifying symbol of the kind Gene Sharp had described.

People commented on the video, quoted the video, even began carrying Zimbabwean flags in solidarity with the ideas expressed in the video. Street vendors started selling Zimbabwean flags too, rushing to satisfy the new demand. A month after he made his first #ThisFlag speech, Mawarire resolved to capitalize on the momentum and to issue one video every day for twenty-five days, hoping that by doing so, he could help start a real discussion about the state of the country. The governor of the Zimbabwean reserve bank agreed to debate him about inflation and about proposed changes to the currency. The tape of that meeting, attended by thousands of #ThisFlag supporters, also went viral. In July, Mawarire called for a national general strike. Millions of people stayed home.

Having first ignored him, then dismissed his video as a "stunt" and his movement as a "pastor's fart in the corridors of power," the regime slowly began to focus on Mawarire as a real threat. Jonathan Moyo, Zimbabwe's minister of information, started an alternative #OurFlag movement in support of the regime. But after it failed to take off, Zimbabwe's leaders moved in a different direction. Instead of merely trumpeting propaganda about the greatness of the leader as a twentieth-century dictator might have done, the regime launched a campaign designed to undermine Mawarire himself: his authenticity, his spontaneity, and especially his patriotism—the very qualities that had galvanized Zimbabweans. To fight back against real emotions, the regime had to portray Mawarire as fake, inauthentic, manipulated by outsiders—not a patriot, but a traitor.

The use of personalized smear campaigns against political opponents is not new. In 64 BC, Cicero's brother Quintus advised him to find dirt on his opponents during his campaign for Roman consul. In the twentieth century, Stalin's regime successfully smeared Trotsky as a traitor and spy, and in the 1930s and 1940s Stalin arrested tens of thousands of other people as Trotsky-sympathizing traitors. But modern autocratic regimes go one step further, for they need to smear not just their opponents but their ideas. To do so, they often frame their language—words like "democracy," "justice," "rule of law"—not as evidence of a genuine, popular, organic desire for change but as evidence of "treason," "foreign links," and of course foreign money.

In 2009, after hundreds of thousands of people objecting to falsified elections joined the largest protests in the Islamic Republic's history, the Iranian authorities fired on demonstrators, arrested the protest leaders, and announced that "we intend to find the link between the plotters and the foreign media." Hugo Chávez repeatedly smeared his opponents as "right-wing" agents of American imperialism, even when those opponents were self-described socialists. The allegation that "George Soros" is organizing demonstrations—the name Soros being a stand-in for "international Jewish conspiracy"—has been used over and over again to smear activists, first by Hungary's autocratic ruling party, then in the United States, Europe, and even Israel. Vladimir Putin threw in a reference to Soros during the press conference he held with Trump in Helsinki in 2018.

At other times he went much further. Putin blamed Hillary Clinton, then the U.S. secretary of state, for demonstrations in Moscow in 2011–12, claiming that she had sent "a signal" to "some actors in our country" and that she had helped funnel hundreds of millions of dollars in "foreign money" to lure protesters into the streets. In 2014, an official Russian website claimed that Ukrainians protesting against a corrupt president were "utilized by masterminds from far away with a sole purpose to turn Ukraine into an 'anti-Russia.'" The historian Marci Shore has written that Russian journalists who visited the Maidan in the winter of 2013–14, when the mass protest was under way, kept asking demonstrators what help they were receiving from Americans. "They simply could not grasp," one young woman explained, "that we ourselves organized ourselves." As Shore explains, "Kremlin propaganda, the conviction that American intelligence or some other world-controlling force must be pulling the strings, betrayed not only malicious intent, but also an inability to believe that there could be such a thing as individuals thinking and acting for themselves."

Following this pattern, the authorities in Zimbabwe attacked Mawarire for allegedly being sponsored by Western governments, citing as evidence retweets and reposts of his statements by foreign embassies. But they also attacked him for alleged financial scams. Mawarire's ordinariness, even his financial struggles, had been a part of his appeal. Moyo and his team therefore portrayed him as a fraudster who "collected money from gullible believers in the United Kingdom, only to evade tax." One government newspaper cited "sources" who claimed that #ThisFlag was "another one of Pastor Mawarire's money spinning ventures."

The public smear campaign was coupled with financial harassment, controls on his movement, and physical violence, though not murder: the point was to scare him and to intimidate his followers, not to make him disappear altogether.

Freedom House has called these kinds of campaigns "civil death." In Zimbabwe, as in so many other places, they are designed to make it impossible to live a productive life. Mawarire was arrested, imprisoned, and tortured. "I can tell you about the interrogation, which went on for hours in the whole night," he told me. "I can't tell you about the torture because of the things they did to me, things I still don't talk about publicly." The pressure included specific threats to his wife and his children, as well as his elderly parents. They kept asking him, "Who's funding you, tell us where you're getting the influence from, how did you get the whole country to strike, did you pay people?" Like the Russian journalists in Ukraine in 2013–14, they simply did not believe anyone could be so idealistic, or perhaps so naive, as to put themselves in danger for "democracy" or for "patriotism." *You will do it just because you love this country? Impossible.*

Mawarire was eventually freed. He sent his family out of the country and then quietly slipped over the border himself.

But instead of diminishing, the campaign against him gained traction. Mawarire presumed people would understand why he had left and would be pleased that he was safe. Zimbabwe's legendary anticolonial revolutionary leaders, Mugabe and Mnangagwa, had spent time in exile too. Instead, some of Mawarire's own supporters began echoing the words of Jonathan Moyo and the mocking, jeering regime media. *See, we told you he was a traitor. See, he's going to live abroad, supported by his paymasters.* "The same social media that built us up," Mawarire told me, "they took us down."

After he left the country, Mawarire told me, he was "consumed by these negative comments. Something in me wanted to prove them wrong. Something in me wanted to say, 'Listen, I'm not a coward.' And secondly, I was genuine about this." He went back to Zimbabwe again and was immediately arrested and strip-searched at the airport. Police took him to a maximum-security prison, where he was beaten again, tortured again, and kept in solitary confinement again. Eventually he was released, and he tried to renew his campaign. He worked to organize people; he set up another general strike, all the while suffering repeated attacks on his integrity, his finances, his intentions. Gradually, it became clear to him that his efforts were in vain. Instead of changing the system, #ThisFlag had alerted the regime to the growing level of discontent, which was adjusting its propaganda accordingly, in 2017 replacing Mugabe with Mnangagwa. Eventually, they offered Mawarire his passport back, and he took the hint. He and his family now live abroad.

"I want to go back to Zimbabwe; who doesn't want to be

back home?" he told me. But he doesn't think he will get there soon: "The first time you get involved, you're so bright-eyed and bushy-tailed and with the belief and hope that it's gonna happen tomorrow—I can see it, I can taste it, we're gonna get it. And then, literally as you have it before you, it vanishes. That's horrible, and then it happens again, and that's when you start to learn that this is gonna take a while."

Instead, he is learning patience.

"I wanted to get it done and get out and go back to being a father. But, you know, the struggle for freedom and democracy is not like that. It draws you in. And then it just . . . it just . . . it remakes you; it reshapes your whole world."

Mawarire had discovered something that many other autocratic governments have now learned: smear campaigns work. When a state apparatus combines the prosecution service, the courts, the police, state-controlled media, and social media in order to frame someone in a particular way—to tell a particular story about their life and their beliefs, to accuse them of treason, fraud, or crime, and sometimes to arrest or torture them as a result of those fake accusations—some fragment of odium always attaches itself to the victim.

In an earlier era, autocratic regimes often solved the problem of dissent simply by murdering dissenters, and some still do. In 2018, Saudi Arabia rid itself of Jamal Khashoggi, a prominent exiled critic and columnist for *The Washington Post,* by murdering him at a Saudi consulate in Istanbul. In 2012, the Cuban government staged a car crash that led to the death of Oswaldo Payá, the most important democratic activist in the country at the time. The Putin regime has murdered a wide range of critics, from the journalist Anna Politkovskaya, in 2006, to the democratic opposition leader Boris Nemtsov, in 2015, to Alexei Navalny, who was poisoned twice and then died in a prison camp in 2024. Chinese police beat Sun Lin, a freelance Chinese journalist, so badly at his home in Nanjing in 2023 that he died a few hours later.

These selective, occasional murders don't just eliminate difficult opponents; they are also a form of messaging. The Saudi monarchy, the Cuban security services, the Kremlin, and the Chinese police don't have to kill every journalist in order to make all journalists in their countries afraid. Modern dictators have learned that the mass violence of the twentieth century is no longer necessary: targeted violence is often enough to keep ordinary people away from politics altogether, convincing them that it's a contest they can never win.

But most of the time, modern autocracies prefer to silence critics without creating corpses. Funerals figure on Gene Sharp's list of nonviolent tactics. Dead heroes can become martyrs. The funeral of László Rajk in 1956 famously helped galvanize what became the Hungarian revolution a few months later. Funerals in apartheid South Africa often turned into powerful anti-regime demonstrations. Funerals in Myanmar serve that function today. The Russian regime was so desperate to avoid a public funeral for Navalny that they tried to blackmail his mother, threatening to let her son's corpse rot unless she promised to bury him in secret; later they refused the family a hearse and restricted entrance to the cemetery. People came anyway, risking arrest, and left mountains of flowers. This is why modern autocrats usually prefer to avoid murder. A martyr can inspire a political movement, while a successful smear campaign can destroy one.

The more sophisticated autocracies now prepare the legal as well as the propaganda basis for these campaigns in advance, creating traps designed to catch democracy activists even before they gain credibility or popularity. Starting in the first decade of the twenty-first century, autocracies and some illiberal democracies began passing laws, often very similar to one another, designed to monitor and control civic organizations, including apolitical and charitable organizations, often by labeling them terrorist, extremist, or treasonous. So-called anti-extremism legislation in Russia has been used to block anyone who expressed political opposition. Yemen passed a series of laws, starting in 2001, apparently copied from laws passed in Egypt, regulating the activities of foreign nongovernmental organizations; similar laws later appeared in Turkey, Eritrea, and Sudan.

In 2009, Uganda passed a law giving a government board the power to regulate and even dissolve domestic civic organizations. An Ethiopian version of the same law gives a similar board the right to abolish organizations if they are deemed "prejudicial to public peace, welfare, or good order in Ethiopia," language sufficiently vague to allow the abolition of almost anything. Cambodia passed a law banning any organizations whose activities "jeopardize peace, stability, and public order or harm the national security, national unity, culture and traditions of Cambodian society," which pretty much covers any activity the government wants to ban. In January 2024, Venezuela's National Assembly took up a new law that would allow the government to dissolve NGOs and impose heavy fines on their members for breaking any of a long list of arbitrary requirements. Cuba, which has not registered any independent organizations since 1985, has recently arrested hundreds of people who participated in informal groups too.

Organizations with genuine foreign links receive even more attention. In 2012, Russia passed laws limiting the rights of NGOs and charities that have foreign funding, requiring them to be publicly labeled "foreign agents," a phrase that sounds, in Russian as in English, a lot like "foreign spies." An illiberal Georgian government tried to pass a very similar law in 2023, dropped the proposal following widespread street demonstrations, and then defied mass opposition to take it up again in 2024. Egypt has likewise conducted criminal investigations into the "foreign funding" of civic organizations. Sudan used laws on security to arrest and detain NGO leaders and to prosecute them for "terrorism." The Belarusian regime detained and searched the homes of the leaders of an organization created to help people with disabilities, again searching for evidence of suspect "foreign funding." In 2016, China passed a law giving the security services the responsibility for registration and oversight of organizations with overseas links, including any health, welfare, or cultural charities that have any connection to the Chinese diaspora.

Most of these measures serve as a false nod to the rule of law, helping justify what comes next, which is often not a political accusation but a false allegation of corruption. Regimes that are themselves profoundly corrupt reverse the charges, blurring the distinction between themselves and their opponents. Back in 2014, Alexei Navalny and his brother were accused of corrupt dealings with a French cosmetics company, Yves Rocher. The case was convoluted and hard to understand; nevertheless, both he and his brother went to prison for it. In 2022 he was given a nine-year sentence for "fraud" as well. Leopoldo López, at the time one of the most popular leaders of the democratic opposition in Venezuela, was in 2008 barred from holding office after the regime accused him of financial crimes; nearly a decade later, in 2017, Henrique Capriles was also barred from running for president using similar accusations.

Even when these charges are false or exaggerated, and even if most people know they are false or exaggerated, they still have an impact. When someone is repeatedly vilified, it is hard even for their closest friends not to think that there must be *some* kernel of truth. When something "secret" is revealed about an activist or political figure, perhaps through publication of a taped conversation or a hacked email—a tactic deployed in Russia since the 1990s, in Poland in 2014, and in the U.S. elections, through the hacking of the Democratic National Committee, in 2016—it creates an impression that the person is dishonest and has something to hide, even when the tape or the hacked email contains no evidence of wrongdoing.

Corruption accusations against dissidents also deflect attention away from the corruption of the ruling party. When the Venezuelan regime, with its links to drug traffickers and organized crime, accuses López of corruption—or when the infamously corrupt Myanmar army leaders leveled similar accusations against Aung San Suu Kyi—part of the purpose is to undermine their popular anticorruption campaigns. However fantastical or hypocritical they may be, corruption allegations also deepen the natural cynicism that autocracies cultivate in their citizens, reinforcing the public's conviction that all politics is dirty, including opposition politics, and that all politicians, even dissident politicians, should be treated with suspicion.

Rather than embracing hope and demanding change, the citizens of Zimbabwe learned from Mawarire's experience to stay away from politics, to treat all politicians, public figures, and potential leaders as equally dangerous, equally dubious, and equally untrustworthy. Indeed, the allegations of corruption against Mawarire might have given some Zimbabweans comfort, because they seemed to give cover to decisions made by ordinary people. Anyone who had ever been bribed into obedience might have felt a kind of reassurance: *See, they are in it for the money too, like me.*

The most sophisticated modern smear campaigns have one additional purpose: they encourage new forms of mass participation. At the height of the Cultural Revolution in Mao's China, workplaces and schools were encouraged to identify class enemies and conduct struggle sessions, during which the enemies were accused of real or imagined thought crimes, humiliated, and sometimes beaten and tortured by their colleagues and classmates. But Maoist struggle sessions took place in a single room. The internet now makes it possible for anyone to join, even anonymously. Participants can contribute their own original memes and slogans, reveling in xenophobic or misogynist themes that would otherwise be taboo.

Sometimes the state organizes the campaign, and others follow voluntarily. Sometimes participants are paid. The Venezuelan government set up a system to transfer small amounts of money to people who retweet or repost government propaganda. The Saudi government has deployed thousands of real and fake Twitter accounts to attack its enemies. Known as the "army of flies," these swarms include both government-run accounts and enthusiastic volunteers. Thanks to this public-private partnership, the Arabic hashtag "We all trust in Mohammed bin Salman" appeared more than 1.1 million times in the wake of the murder of Khashoggi. The sense of power and connection that people once got from joining crowds can now be experienced at home, at a laptop, or on a phone, behind closed doors.

The pain, anxiety, and paranoia that this new kind of mob campaign can inflict, especially when they are directed by a state that also controls the police and the security services, can be overwhelming. Anyone subjected to a mass, online trolling campaign, especially one backed by the state, becomes toxic, even to family and close friends. López, the Venezuelan leader who spent seven years either in prison or under house arrest—and is now, like Mawarire, in exile—told me that after a long absence he paid a visit to one of his oldest, closest friends. After speaking to him for a few minutes, she began to cry. "Forgive me," she said, "but we doubted. We believed what they were saying about you." Other friends told López that when they wrote or posted in his defense online, they were overwhelmed: "It's just incredible, the machinery of trolls who come out of the woodwork." And it's not just trolling they fear. In Venezuela—as in Zimbabwe, Russia, Iran, or China—the regime can also use financial investigations, pressure on spouses and employers, low-level threats, or even real violence, not just against opponents, but against their supporters, friends, and family.

Having experienced this himself, López told me that he now warns colleagues in Venezuela and other countries who become the center of opposition protests to "get ready for when the protests fade away"—to prepare themselves for what could come next and not to take it personally, because this is now a familiar pattern. A form of public despair will often follow the crushing of an opposition movement, especially if violence has been used. People will mourn the dead and wounded. They will feel bitter because they have lost hope.

After that they will be angry. They will be angry because the situation is worse, because their hopes have been dashed, and because their leaders have disappointed them.

To the inhabitants of most modern democracies, the stories of López and Mawarire may sound horrific and cruel. At the same time, descriptions of online mobs, targeted smear campaigns, and the creation of fake charges and false narratives might also sound familiar. Technologies built in Silicon Valley and public relations tactics invented on Madison Avenue long ago meshed with dictatorial behavior to create coordinated online harassment campaigns that are widely used not just by amateur online activists, and not just in "cancellation" campaigns or online pile-ons, but by democratically elected governments and leaders around the world. Indeed, they are often a flashing signal of democratic decline.

Certainly that was the case in 2020, when a professional troll, hired by a deputy justice minister and member of what was then Poland's ruling party, the national-populist Law and Justice, set out to harass judges whose rulings and public comments were critical of government policy. She sent vulgar postcards to the chief justice of Poland's supreme court and defamatory information about another judge to all his colleagues, as well as to the judge himself. She posted material about judges too ("Fuck off," she wrote in one post: "You are bringing shame on honest judges and dishonor to Poland"). Her efforts, revealed only because she described them to a news website, were a small part of the government's broader campaign to undermine the judiciary as an institution, and rule of law more broadly.

The campaign against Denise Dresser, a Mexican political scientist, columnist, feminist, and activist, had some of the same qualities. Starting in 2020, the president of Mexico, Andrés Manuel López Obrador, regularly attacked her at the press conferences he held every morning. Dresser was a left-wing critic of the president; because López Obrador also styled himself as a man of the left, he might have felt especially threatened by her criticism of his government's attempts to politicize Mexico's judiciary and its electoral commission. His response was to frame Dresser as "elite," as a "conservative," as someone who is "against the people," and, of course, as a traitor.

The president's online trolls—some clearly professional, others probably spontaneous volunteers—took the attacks further. They called Dresser old, ugly, irrelevant, crazy, menopausal. They invented or elaborated stories about her divorce and other aspects of her personal life. They created memes showing her in a straitjacket. When she wrote in support of Ukraine, she was depicted as a bomb-carrying "warmonger." People took surreptitious photographs of her in public places; one of those photos, taken at a Starbucks, seemed to show the top of her dress unzipped. That picture went viral, with commentary about how Dresser lived alone and had dementia.

People also sent threats, which she had to take seriously. In 2022, Mexico was the most dangerous country for reporters in the world outside actual war zones, and the possibility of violence—from drug gangs, other criminals, and enraged fans of the president—is very real. Putin can give explicit orders to have people murdered. Illiberal leaders like López Obrador and Jarosław Kaczyński, the leader of Poland's Law and Justice Party, simply drive hatred in someone's direction and wait to see what happens. In Poland, a smear campaign directed at the mayor of Gdańsk, Paweł Adamowicz, ended tragically in 2019 when a man who had been watching state television in jail rushed onto a stage at a public event and stabbed the mayor with a knife. Adamowicz died a few hours later.

In the past, the American government has also abused its powers to target individuals. The FBI successfully bugged, harassed, and manipulated Dr. Martin Luther King Jr. President Richard Nixon sought, unsuccessfully, to use the IRS to make life difficult for his enemies. There is not—at least not as of this writing—an example of the contemporary American federal government using all the instruments of the state—legal, judicial, financial—in combination with a modern, online hate campaign to target one of the president's personal enemies. But it is not difficult to imagine how this could happen.

Both as president and afterward, Donald Trump has sought to stoke anger and even violence against people he dislikes, including federal judges. He and his followers harassed election workers across the country who refused to go along with his fraudulent accusations about a stolen election. He published the telephone number of the Michigan Senate majority leader, who subsequently received four thousand threatening text messages, as well as the personal information of the speaker of the Pennsylvania House of Representatives, which led protesters to show up at his home. He and his team falsely accused two Georgia poll workers, Shaye Moss and her mother, Ruby Freeman, of stuffing suitcases with illegal ballots, an allegation that led to months of often racist harassment. In 2023, Trump began talking about using the Department of Justice to arrest his enemies, not because they are guilty of something, but because, if he returns to the presidency, he wants "retribution." If he ever succeeds in directing federal courts and law enforcement at his enemies, in combination with a mass trolling campaign, then the blending of the autocratic and democratic worlds will be complete.

Epilogue

Democrats United

Vladimir Putin's Black Sea palace has a hockey rink and a hookah bar. Xi Jinping lives and works on the grounds of what used to be an imperial garden. Dictators around the world meet in drawing rooms with gilded chandeliers and marble fireplaces.

Democrats meet in a rambling hotel outside Vilnius, with dark corridors and windows overlooking a forest. In the autumn of 2022, that was the site of the first-ever meeting of the World Liberty Congress, a gathering of people who have fought autocracies all around the world. Politicians and activists from Russia, Zimbabwe, Iran, South Sudan, North Korea, Nicaragua, Rwanda, Cuba, and China met in rooms with long tables and bad lighting, encountering colleagues from Venezuela, Syria, Cambodia, Belarus, and Uganda.

The modest surroundings masked a wealth of experience. I struck up a conversation with a young man in a tweed jacket. "You probably think I am from Hong Kong," he said. He was wearing wire-rimmed spectacles and spoke the clipped English common in former British colonies. Yes, I told him, I did think he was from Hong Kong. "I'm from North Korea," he said. This was Timothy Cho. Abandoned by his parents at nine, Cho grew up homeless, escaped from North Korea twice, was imprisoned four times, and, when I met him, was trying to become a Conservative Party parliamentary candidate in the U.K.

Earlier that day, Bobi Wine, a Ugandan musician and nearly successful presidential candidate—or maybe, if the votes had been counted correctly, a genuinely successful one—spoke to the group. He argued against the use of the word "opposition." No, he argued, we are not an *opposition;* we are an *option,* a better option: "We should adopt positive language. We are not victims." In the evening, I spoke with a pair of Russians who prefer to remain anonymous. They were running a stealth campaign against military mobilization, helping get lawyers and legal advice to Russians who want to avoid the draft. They had made the momentous decision not to leave Russia, because they thought that persuading people not to fight was the best thing they could do to help end the war against Ukraine.

Most of the participants were meeting one another for the first time. Even some from the same continent didn't know one another, except by name or reputation. In Africa, one of them told me, commerce and conversation with Europeans two thousand miles away can be easier than with fellow Africans on the other side of the border. But when they do speak, they discover that they have similar experiences, have been exposed to similar smear campaigns, and have lived under similar regimes whose leaders launder money and talk about "multipolarity" in similar ways. To them, Autocracy, Inc., isn't a book title: it's a reality that they grapple with every day. By sharing experiences, they learn to understand the patterns, to anticipate the tactics that will be used against them, and to prepare to resist them.

Nine months earlier, I had sat in the upstairs room of a New York restaurant while a smaller group of exiled politicians planned the Vilnius summit. López, the Venezuelan opposition leader, began by reminding everyone in the room that although autocrats work together to keep one another in power, there is "no alliance of those of us who are fighting for freedom." Garry Kasparov, the chess champion and advocate for political change in Russia, believed it was important to show that "we are united, we represent a mass movement, and we have support from the free world." Masih Alinejad, the Iranian activist whose social media campaign persuaded thousands of Iranian women to discard their veils, said she thought that "if we make them hear us and understand us," the combined forces of democracy activists could shape debate in Washington and Silicon Valley: "We are not just fighting for our own people. We are fighting for democracy everywhere, even in the West." All of them wanted to make an impact not only in their own countries but in the democratic world as well. Already, they understood that one nation's freedom can often depend on the strength of freedom in others.

Their language sounded almost like a global version of Gene Sharp's handbook. We are more numerous than they are. We, the proponents of freedom, can drown out the advocates of dictatorship. But they also understand that we no longer live in the era of Gene Sharp. There is no global public square where López, Kasparov, and Alinejad can protest alongside Evan Mawarire of Zimbabwe, Sviatlana Tsikhanouskaya of Belarus, and Rosa María Payá, the daughter of Oswaldo Payá, let alone organize nineteen different kinds of strikes and fourteen other forms of protest. Instead, the translation of their words into something useful requires a different way of thinking about politics altogether. "First," said López, "we have to reframe the problem." And he is right.

Western and especially American students of foreign policy often look at the world as a series of separate issues—eastern Europe, the Middle East, the South China Sea—each requiring a different cadre of experts or specialists. But that isn't how autocracies see the world. Putin backs far-right and extremist movements in Europe and provides thugs and weapons to support African dictatorships. He pursues victory in Ukraine by creating food shortages and raising energy prices around the world. Iran maintains proxies in Lebanon, Palestine, Yemen, and Iraq. Iranian agents have also bombed a Jewish community center in Buenos Aires, carried out murders in Istanbul and Paris, plotted assassinations in the United States, and funded media throughout the Arab-speaking and Spanish-speaking worlds. The Belarusian dictator tried to destabilize his neighbors by luring refugees from the Middle East and helping them cross illegally into Europe. Cuban troops have gone to fight against Ukraine in Russia, while Cuban secret policemen help protect the Maduro regime in Venezuela. China, with deep economic and political interests across Africa and Latin America, has not thought of itself as an "Asian" power for many years.

The autocracies keep track of one another's defeats and victories, timing their own moves to create maximum chaos. In the autumn of 2023, both the European Union and the U.S. Congress found themselves unable to send aid to Ukraine because minorities with deep Russian ties, led respectively by Viktor Orbán in Hungary and by a handful of MAGA Republicans in Congress, many acting under the instructions of Donald Trump, blocked the majority and delayed the aid. A narrative promoting "Ukraine fatigue" spread across the internet, pushed by Russian proxies and Chinese media in multiple languages.

At exactly that moment, Iranian-backed Hamas militants launched a brutal attack on Israel. In the weeks that followed, Iranian-backed Houthi militants began firing on tankers and cargo ships in the Red Sea, disrupting global trade and distracting the United States and Europe from the Ukraine war. The Azeri dictator, Ilham Aliyev, had already made use of the same moment of global distraction to capture the disputed territory of Nagorno-Karabakh and expel 100,000 Armenians, the entire population, in a matter of days. By the spring of 2024, Chinese hackers were discovered to be burrowing deep into the computers and data storage of the British parliament and its members. In Brussels, Warsaw, and Prague, a multinational investigation revealed a broad

Russian influence-buying campaign, including payments to members of the European parliament and attempts to shape European elections.

Meanwhile, in the Western Hemisphere, President Maduro said he was contemplating the invasion and occupation of a province of neighboring Guyana. As he was announcing these plans, hundreds of thousands of Venezuelan citizens, impoverished by Maduro's policies, were trudging through Central America toward the U.S. border. Their unprecedented numbers were helping fuel a populist, xenophobic backlash in the United States and boost support for the MAGA wing of the Republican Party, which was openly backing Putin in his war to destroy Ukraine.

This multifaceted, interconnected, self-reinforcing polycrisis was not coordinated by a single mastermind, and it is not evidence of a secret conspiracy. Instead, these episodes, taken together, demonstrate how different autocracies have extended their influence across different political, economic, military, and informational spheres. They also show how much damage they can do when they opportunistically work together toward their common goal: damaging democracies and democratic values, inside their own countries and around the world. Read, once again, the statement of Xi Jinping and Vladimir Putin on February 4, 2022, on the eve of the Russian invasion of Ukraine. They denounced "interference in the internal affairs of sovereign states under the pretext of protecting democracy and human rights." They called upon the outside world "to respect cultural and civilizational diversity and the rights of peoples of different countries to self-determination." And they warned, angrily, that any discussion of democratic standards, which they called "attempts at hegemony," would "pose serious threats to global and regional peace and stability and undermine the stability of the world order."

Others have used even more brutal, more extreme language, openly calling for mass atrocities or war—language that no one in the democratic world has yet taken seriously or begun to counter. During a meeting with Putin in September 2023, the North Korean dictator, Kim Jong Un, offered his full and unconditional support for Russia's "sacred fight to punish the gathering of evil that claims hegemony." A few months later, in January 2024, Kim appeared to abandon his own past attempts at reconciliation, calling for a constitutional change that would identify democratic South Korea as North Korea's principal enemy, dismantling all the institutions that had promoted unification and cross-border exchange, warning of a war that would "destroy the entity called the Republic of Korea and terminate its existence." In the same week, Dmitry Medvedev, a former president and former prime minister of Russia, called Ukraine a "cancerous growth" and called for the destruction not just of the current Ukrainian government but of "any version of Ukraine whatsoever." Not long afterward, he produced a map of Russia that incorporated almost all of modern Ukraine and distributed most of the rest of Ukrainian territory to Poland and Hungary.

Still, I began with the idea that we are not living through a new Cold War, a "Cold War 2.0," and I want to underscore that statement again. In no sense is the modern competition between autocratic and democratic ideas and practices a direct replica of what we faced in the twentieth century. There are no "blocs" to join and no Berlin Walls marking neat geographic divides. Many countries don't fit comfortably into either category, democracy or autocracy. As I've written, some autocracies—the U.A.E., Saudi Arabia, Singapore, Vietnam—seek cooperation with the democratic world, don't want to upend the UN Charter, and still see the advantages of international law. Some democracies—Turkey, Israel, Hungary, India, the Philippines—have elected leaders who are more inclined to break conventions on human rights than to uphold them. Because autocratic alliances are largely transactional, they can shift and change, and often do.

The divisions run inside countries, too. There are powerful and important democracy movements in Venezuela and Iran. There are significant autocratic political movements and politicians in the United States as well as Germany, Poland, the Netherlands, Italy, and France. At the same time, the world economy is far more complex than it was in the twentieth century, and it is pointless to pretend that there are no conflicts of interest. Global cooperation will be needed to mitigate climate change and other environmental challenges. The United States and Europe trade intensively with China, and it is neither easy nor desirable to end those trading links abruptly.

For all these reasons, the democracies of North America, Latin America, Europe, Asia, and Africa, together with the leaders of the democratic opposition in Russia, China, Iran,

Venezuela, Cuba, Belarus, Zimbabwe, Myanmar, and other autocratic states, should think about the struggle for freedom not as a competition with specific autocratic states, and certainly not as "war with China," but as a war against autocratic *behaviors,* wherever they are found: in Russia, in China, in Europe, in the United States. Toward this end, we need networks of lawyers and public officials to fight corruption inside our own countries and around the world, in cooperation with the democratic activists who understand kleptocracy best. We need military and intelligence coalitions that can anticipate and halt lawless violence. We need economic warriors in multiple countries who can track the impact of sanctions in real time, understand who is breaking them, and take steps to stop them. We need people willing to organize online and coordinate campaigns to identify and debunk dehumanizing propaganda. The autocracies want to create a global system that benefits thieves, criminals, dictators, and the perpetrators of mass murder. We can stop them.

Put an End to Transnational Kleptocracy

A Russian, Angolan, or Chinese oligarch can own a house in London, an estate on the Mediterranean, a company in Delaware, and a trust in South Dakota without ever having to reveal ownership to tax authorities anywhere. American and European intermediaries—lawyers, bankers, accountants, real estate agents, and public relations and "reputation management" advisers—make these kinds of transactions possible. Their work is legal. We have made it so. We can just as easily make it illegal. All of it. We don't need to tolerate a little bit of corruption. We can simply end the whole system.

We could, for example, require all real estate transactions, everywhere in the United States and Europe, to be totally transparent. We could require all companies to be registered in the name of their actual owners, and all trusts to reveal the names of their beneficiaries. We could ban our own citizens from keeping money in jurisdictions that promote secrecy, and we could ban lawyers and accountants from engaging with them. That doesn't mean that they would cease to exist, but they would be much harder to use. We could close loopholes that allow anonymity in the private-equity and hedge-fund industries too. We could create effective enforcement teams and then help them operate across countries and continents. We could do all this in coordination with other partners around the world.

There will be enormous resistance: if the dismantling of this system were easy, it would have happened already. Money-laundering mechanisms are hard to understand and even harder to police. Anonymous transactions can move through different bank accounts in different countries in a matter of seconds, while anyone seeking to follow the money and understand what happened may need years to find out. Governments are often ambivalent about prosecuting powerful people. Civil servants charged with tracking complex, secretive billion-dollar deals earn low salaries themselves, and may not want to target people with much greater wealth and influence. Powerful people benefit from the existing system, want to keep it in place, and have deep connections across the political spectrum. Sheldon Whitehouse, a U.S. senator who has argued for greater financial transparency for many years, once told me that he does so partly because "the same techniques of concealment used to facilitate offshore thugs and criminal activities also facilitate the political activities of domestic special interests." The individuals who benefit from financial secrecy often seek direct political influence, and this too makes them hard to block. Ihor Kolomoisky, the Ukrainian oligarch who hid his money in property schemes all over the American Midwest, reportedly sought to preserve his empire by angling for influence in the Trump administration, including by offering the president "dirt" on Joe and Hunter Biden, some of which was passed to Donald Trump's personal lawyer, Rudy Giuliani. Kolomoisky has claimed the opposite—that he was revealing this story, not feeding it—but that could well have been a means of seeking influence in the Biden administration.

For all those reasons, no single politician, party, or country can reform this system alone. Instead, an international coalition will have to change the laws, end secretive practices, and restore transparency to the international financial system. An anti-kleptocracy network could include those Treasury and finance ministry officials from across Europe, Asia, and North America who have begun to understand how much damage money laundering and dark money have done to their own economies. They could work with community leaders from London, Vancouver, Miami, and other cities whose landscapes, property markets, and economies have been distorted by Russians, Angolans, Venezuelans, and Chinese buying property that they use as a means of storing wealth.

The coalition could also include the activists who know more about how money is stolen in their own countries than outsiders, and more about how to communicate that information. Alexei Navalny was murdered by the Russian state precisely because he was so good at both. In the years before his final arrest, Navalny made a series of crowdfunded documentary films, posted on YouTube, that tied the leaders of Russia to far-reaching financial scams and broad networks of enablers. The videos succeeded because they were professionally made, because they included shocking details—the hookah bar and hockey rink inside Putin's vulgar Black Sea residence, as well as the vineyard, the helicopter pad, and the oyster farm—and because they linked these stories to the poverty of Russian teachers, doctors, and civil servants. *You have bad roads and bad health care,* Navalny told Russians, *because they have vineyards and oyster farms.*

This was investigative journalism but packaged and designed to move people—to explain to them the connection between the palaces built by distant rulers and themselves—and it worked. Some of the videos received hundreds of millions of views. Now imagine the same project, but backed by democratic governments, media, and activists around the world. Not just investigations, and not just prosecutions, but campaigns to publicize them and to connect them to ordinary people's lives. Just as the democratic world once built an international anticommunist alliance, so can the United States and its allies build an international anticorruption alliance, organized around the idea of transparency, accountability, and fairness, enhanced by the creative thinking found in the autocratic diasporas as well as the democracies themselves.

Don't Fight the Information War—Undermine It

Modern autocrats take information and ideas seriously. They understand the importance not only of controlling opinion inside their own countries but also of influencing debates around the world. They spend accordingly: on television outlets, local and national newspapers, troll networks. They court politicians and business leaders in democratic countries in order to have local mouthpieces and advocates. They work together to amplify the same conspiracy theories and the same themes across different platforms.

During the three decades that have passed since the end of the Cold War, the United States and its allies imagined that they had no need to compete in this sphere, because good information would somehow win the battle in the "marketplace of ideas." But there isn't a marketplace of ideas, or in any case not a free market of ideas. Instead, some ideas have been turbocharged by disinformation campaigns, by heavy spending by the social media companies whose algorithms promote emotional and divisive content, and perhaps, in some cases, by algorithms designed to promote Russian or Chinese narratives in a similar manner. Since we first encountered Russian disinformation inside our own societies, we've imagined that our existing forms of communication could beat it without any special effort. But no one who studies autocratic propaganda believes that fact-checking or even swift reactions are sufficient. By the time the correction is made, the falsehood has already traveled around the world. Our old models never acknowledged the truth that many people *desire* disinformation. They are attracted by conspiracy theories and will not necessarily seek out reliable news at all.

We can begin to fight back, first, by understanding that we are facing an epidemic of information laundering and by exposing it when we can. In 2023, the U.S. government began to do exactly that. The State Department's Global Engagement Center (GEC) marshaled intelligence and information collected by the rest of the government and began to expose a series of planned Russian campaigns *before* they took place, a tactic that James Rubin, who has run the GEC since 2022, calls "pre-bunking." The GEC revealed the campaign to spread disinformation about health in Africa, identifying the names of Russians involved, and then informed media in the African countries most affected. The GEC also exposed the Russian plan to coordinate disinformation in Latin America, using Pressenza and other websites, and informed Spanish-language media too. The French government, together with several EU institutions, have exposed RRN, the group that created the "typosquatting" network in France and Germany. The German government revealed another operation aimed at German speakers, including some fifty thousand fake Twitter accounts that sent out more than a million messages during a one-month period in late 2023, many insinuating that the German government was neglecting Germans by providing weapons and aid for Ukraine. By describing these campaigns in advance, the American, French, and German governments hope to alert some people, at least, to their existence.

Of course the problem runs deeper: none of these campaigns would have any chance of success if the social media platforms that host them were not so easy to game. Reform of these platforms is a vast topic, with implications that range well beyond foreign policy, and the resistance even to a civilized discussion of social media regulation is enormous. The platforms are among the wealthiest and most influential companies in the world and, like the companies that benefit from money laundering, they lobby against change; so do many politicians, especially on the far right, who find the current system amenable. Together, they have prevented any productive debate, even as online conversation has grown markedly worse. After Elon Musk purchased Twitter, the platform quickly became a more powerful amplifier of extremist, antisemitic, and pro-Russian narratives. TikTok, the Chinese-built platform, remains a potent and badly understood source of misinformation, not least because it is entirely untransparent. If it is being used to shape U.S. politics, or to collect data from users, we don't know how. The American far right has meanwhile shifted the legitimate political debate about online platform regulation into an argument about "bans" and "free speech," attacking the academics and other researchers who seek to understand how the online world functions and to explore how it could be made more transparent.

But just like the financial system, the information system is based on a series of laws, rules, and regulations, all of which can be changed, if our politicians are prepared to change them. Transparency can replace obscurity. Customers of the social media platforms should be able to own their own data and determine what is done with it. They should also be able to influence, directly, the algorithms that determine what they see. Legislators in democracies could create the technical and legal means to give people more control and more choices or to hold companies liable if the algorithms they use promote content tied to acts of terrorism. Citizen-scientists should be able to work with the platforms in order to better understand their impact, just as citizen-scientists in the past worked with food companies to ensure better hygiene or with oil companies to prevent environmental damage.

Like the fight against kleptocracy, the fight for evidence-based conversations requires broader international coalitions. The United States and its allies may need to join forces with one another and with media companies to make Reuters, the Associated Press, and other reliable outlets the standard source of global news instead of Xinhua and RT. Joint action, taken by governments as well as private companies, might be required to ensure that Chinese programming and Chinese news sources are not always the cheapest option in Africa or Latin America. No democratic government should ever assume that arguments for democracy or for the rule of law are somehow obvious or self-evident. Authoritarian narratives are designed to undermine the innate appeal of those ideas, to characterize dictatorship as stable and democracy as chaotic. Democratic media, civic organizations, and politicians need to argue back and make the case for transparency, accountability, and liberty—at home and around the world.

A joint effort can also help the citizens of autocracies better understand the global context of their regimes. If the Russian diaspora, the Hong Kong diaspora, the Venezuelan diaspora, and the Iranian diaspora can amplify one another's messages and ideas, then together they can have a larger impact than any individual group could have by itself. In some places, this has been tried. Kloop, the now-banned Kyrgyz news organization, successfully worked for years to create links among independent journalists in central Asia so that even people in very closed countries can better understand what is happening in the region, including the Russian attempts to dominate their information space. Several Russian independent websites, such as Meduza and the Insider, now translate their best investigative reporting into English so that it can reach wider audiences around the world. At open and private meetings like the one I attended outside Vilnius, activists in the autocratic world already exchange experiences, plan joint strategies, and teach one another how to access blocked websites. If we back them, they can help one another communicate better information, more convincingly, and then they can teach us.

Unlike their twentieth-century predecessors, today's autocrats cannot impose censorship easily or effectively. Instead, they have focused on winning audiences, building support for their messages by channeling resentment, hatred, and the desire for superiority. We have to learn to compete while preserving and promoting our own values. That means breaking the autocrats' monopoly on the use of strong emotions, connecting to audiences with the issues that concern them the most, and above all showing how the fight for truth leads to change. Journalists who uncover corruption need to work with lawyers and sanctions advocates to ensure their investigations lead to punishment. Good information has to help bring positive change. Truth has to be seen to lead to justice.

Decouple, De-risk, Rebuild

On September 26, 2022, fifty-five years after the meeting in the Habsburg hunting lodge, the European experiment in autocratic-democratic interdependence came to an end. First one massive underwater explosion, then several others, ripped through the Nord Stream 2 pipeline. Three out of the four individual pipes were destroyed, and the $20 billion project was rendered useless. Along with the physical pipeline, this act of sabotage destroyed the idea that Germans, Europeans, or Americans could promote democracy through trade.

From the very beginning, the Russians intended Nord Stream 2 to have the opposite purpose: Russia hoped to promote kleptocracy in Germany and to set the stage for Russian domination of Ukraine. The pipeline was meant to transport gas directly from Russia to Germany, bypassing Poland and Ukraine, making it possible to cut those countries out of lucrative transit deals and perhaps to cut off Ukraine's gas supplies altogether. Even before the agreement was signed, Russia had already begun using gas pricing and gas availability as a tool of political influence, cutting off Ukraine from gas supplies in 2005–6 and again in 2014, fixing prices, and playing political games around gas in central and eastern Europe.

The pipeline also became the basis for a new kind of special relationship between Russia and Germany. The Russian companies involved in Nord Stream became enmeshed in German culture and politics. Gazprom helped finance an exhibition at the German Historical Museum in Berlin, devoted to an idealized version of Russian-German history, and became a cosponsor of Schalke, a German soccer club that happened to be the favorite of the German president and former foreign minister, Frank-Walter Steinmeier. The companies also had close links to German and Russian politicians. Matthias Warnig, a former Stasi officer who had been stationed in Dresden at the same time as Putin, became Nord Stream's chief executive. Gerhard Schröder, the chancellor who had agreed to the construction of Nord Stream, accepted Putin's suggestion that he become the head of the Nord Stream AG shareholders' committee only a few days after leaving office. By 2022, the year Russia invaded Ukraine, Schröder was earning close to $1 million annually from companies connected to the pipeline and to Russian gas, Rosneft among them. Not all the relationships that grew up around the pipeline were corrupt (and Schröder emphatically denied that his were). But neither did they turn out to be compatible with Germany's national interest or with Europe's strategic stability. When, even after the first invasion of Ukraine in

2014, Chancellor Angela Merkel, Schröder's successor, did not put an end to the Nord Stream project, Putin might have come to believe he had a green light to continue his invasion.

Many have speculated about Merkel's motives, but in fact her views were the same as those of virtually every other democratic leader in her era. She believed that mutually beneficial investments and a bit of patience would encourage Russia to integrate with Europe, just as Europeans had learned to integrate after World War II. She failed to understand that Russian companies were acting not as private companies but as agents of the Russian state, representing the interests of the Kremlin in myriad commercial and political transactions. She did not understand the potential hazards of trade with the Chinese companies that are sometimes subsidized or directed by the Chinese Communist Party either, or the danger of relying upon them for everything from rare minerals to medical supplies.

The risks of overdependence on trade with Russia, China, or other autocracies aren't just economic. They are existential. Following the invasion of Ukraine, Europeans learned the hard way how high a price they had paid for their decision to rely upon Russian gas. The shift to more expensive energy sources caused inflation. Inflation in turn caused dissatisfaction. Compounded by a Russian disinformation campaign, this dissatisfaction contributed to a surge in support for the German far right, a political movement that would alter the nature of postwar Germany beyond recognition, if it ever took power.

In April 2023, Jake Sullivan, President Biden's national

security adviser, spoke to a Washington audience about the risks that a similar kind of overdependence on China might eventually pose. His argument was not for *decoupling*—meaning the total detachment of the U.S. economy from China's—but for *de-risking:* ensuring that the United States and the rest of the democratic world do not remain dependent on China for anything that could be weaponized in case of a crisis. He gave some examples, pointing out that the United States "produces only 4 percent of the lithium, 13 percent of the cobalt, 0 percent of the nickel, and 0 percent of the graphite required to meet current demand for electric vehicles. Meanwhile, more than 80 percent of critical minerals are processed by one country, China." He went on to advocate for the construction of a "clean-energy manufacturing ecosystem rooted in supply chains here in North America, and extending to Europe, Japan, and elsewhere."

This case needs to be made more dramatically, for the democratic world's dependence on China, Russia, and other autocracies for minerals, semiconductors, or energy supplies poses more than just an economic risk. Those business relationships are corrupting our own societies. Russia has been using its pipelines not, as the German chancellor Willy Brandt once hoped, to deepen commercial ties and help consolidate a lasting peace in Europe but to wield a weapon of blackmail, to influence European politics in Russia's favor. Chinese businesses use their presence around the world to collect data and information that could eventually help them wage cyberwarfare. Russian, Chinese, and other oligarchic money in American and British real estate has distorted property markets in major cities and corrupted more than one politician. The fact that anonymous shell companies were purchasing condominiums in Trump-branded properties while Trump was president should have set off alarm bells. That it did not is evidence of how accustomed to kleptocratic corruption we have become.

Our trading relationships with Autocracy, Inc., carry other risks too. Ursula von der Leyen, the president of the European Commission, also gave a speech in the spring of 2023, arguing that the economic relationship between China and Europe "is unbalanced and increasingly affected by distortions created by China's state capitalist system." To put it more bluntly, the Chinese government subsidizes its largest companies to help them compete. Her call to "rebalance this relationship on the basis of transparency, predictability, and reciprocity" was a polite way of saying that we need tariffs, bans, and export controls to ensure China cannot undercut our industries using government funds.

This warning could also go further, for the competition is not only with China, and not only in trade. We may now be at an inflection point, a moment when we have to decide how to shape surveillance technology, artificial intelligence, the Internet of Things, voice- or face-recognition systems, and other emerging technologies so that their inventors and their users remain accountable to democratic laws, as well as to principles of human rights and standards of transparency. We have already failed to regulate social media, with negative consequences for politics around the world. Failure to regulate AI before it distorts political conversations, just to take one obvious example, could have a catastrophic impact over time. Democracies should work, again in coalitions, to promote transparency, to create international standards, to ensure that autocracies don't set the rules and shape the products.

We are becoming aware of all these things very late. Around the world, democratic activists, from Moscow to Hong Kong to Caracas, have been warning us that our industries, our economic policies, and our research efforts are enabling the economic and even the military aggression of others, and they are right.

Some of the wealthiest and most powerful Americans and Europeans are themselves playing ambivalent roles in these trades. We no longer live in a world where the very wealthy can do business with autocratic regimes, sometimes promoting the foreign policy goals of those regimes, while at the same time doing business with the American government, or with European governments, and enjoying the status and privileges of citizenship and legal protection in the free markets of the democratic world. It's time to make them choose.

Democrats United

"Democrats united": I use this phrase with care. I don't intend it to be an insult, or to imply that the democratic world should become a mirror of the autocratic world. On the contrary, I am using it because I believe the citizens of the United States, and the citizens of the democracies of Europe, Asia, Africa, and Latin America, should begin thinking of themselves as linked to one another and to the people who share their values inside autocracies too. They need one another, now more than ever, because their democracies are not safe. Nobody's democracy is safe.

Americans, with our long history of imagining ourselves to be exceptional, would do well to remember that our domestic politics have always been connected to, and influenced by, a larger struggle for freedom and the rule of law around the world. Europeans who aspire to a Fortress Europe also need to wake up to the reality that Russian influence campaigns and Chinese commercial interests are already shaping their politics and limiting their choices. We are used to thinking of "the West" influencing the world, but nowadays the influence often runs the other way. Even if we don't believe it or don't acknowledge it, that won't make it go away.

Most Parisians, Madrileños, New Yorkers, and Londoners do not have strong feelings about the political leaders of Russia, China, Iran, and Venezuela. But those rulers pay close attention to what happens in Paris, Madrid, New York, and London. They understand that the language of democracy, anticorruption, and justice—language we often use without thinking about it—poses dangers to their power. They will continue to try to mold our politics and our economics to their advantage, even if we cover our eyes and ears and refuse to notice, as many would prefer.

Isolationism is an instinctive and even understandable reaction to the ugliness of the modern interconnected world. For some politicians in democracies, it will continue to offer a successful path to power. The campaign for Brexit succeeded by using the metaphor "take back control," and no wonder: everyone wants more control in a world where events on the other side of the planet can affect jobs and prices in our local towns and villages. But did the removal of Britain from the European Union give the British more power to shape the world? Did it prevent foreign money from shaping U.K. politics? Did it stop refugees from moving from the war zones of the Middle East to Britain? It did not.

The temptation of what is sometimes called realism—the belief that nations are solely motivated by a struggle for power, that they have eternal interests and permanent geopolitical orientations—is as strong as that of isolationism, and can be equally misleading, not least because it appeals to the indifferent. If nations never change, then of course we don't need to exert the effort to make them change. If nations have permanent orientations, then all we need to do is discover what those are and get used to them. If nothing else, the Ukraine war showed us that nations are not pieces in a game of Risk. Their behavior can be altered by acts of cowardice or bravery, by wise leaders and cruel ones, and above all by good ideas and bad ones. Their interactions are not inevitable; their alliances and enmities are not permanent. There was no coalition to aid Ukraine until February 2022, and then there was. That coalition then made what had appeared to be the inevitable, rapid conquest of Ukraine impossible. By the same token, a different kind of Russian leader, with a different set of ideas, could now end the war quickly.

There is no liberal world order anymore, and the aspiration to create one no longer seems real. But there are liberal societies, open and free countries that offer a better chance for people to live useful lives than closed dictatorships do. They are hardly perfect. Those that exist have deep flaws, profound divisions, and terrible historical scars. But that's all the more reason to defend and protect them. So few of them have existed across human history; so many have existed for a short time and then failed. They can be destroyed from the outside and from the inside, too, by division and demagogues. Or they can be saved. But only if those of us who live in them are willing to make the effort to save them.

Acknowledgments

The title of this book, *Autocracy, Inc.,* comes from a conversation with the democracy activist and deep thinker Srdja Popovic, whose work is an important inspiration for me as for so many other people. Conversations with Yevgenia Albats, Ladan Boroumand, James Bosworth, Thomas Carothers, Nick Donovan, Denise Dresser, Steven Feldstein, Garry Kasparov, Joshua Kurlantzick, Leopoldo López, Evan Mawarire, Rosa María Payá, Peter Pomerantsev, Alexander Sikorski, Radek Sikorski, Tadeusz Sikorski, Svitlana Tsikhanouskaya, Christopher Walker, Jack Watling, Damon Wilson, and Tammy Wittes also contributed to the ideas in this book. Lisa Shymko and the Peterson Literary Fund were early supporters of my research.

Cullen Murphy was an important early reader and editor, Francisco Toro an equally important later adviser and editor. Abigail Skalka helped with research. Reuel Marc Gerecht, Christopher Walker, Peter Pomerantsev, and Andrea Kendall-Taylor all read parts of the manuscript. Jeffrey Goldberg and

Scott Stossel commissioned and edited the original *Atlantic* article, "The Bad Guys Are Winning," which became the introduction to this book. Dante Ramos edited most of the dozen-odd other *Atlantic* articles that I drew upon when writing this book as well. Lisa Shymko and the Peterson Literary Fund were early supporters of my research.

Special thanks are owed to an unusual trio: Stuart Proffitt, my British editor; Kris Puopolo, my American editor; and Georges Borchardt, my literary agent, all of whom have now worked with me for more than two decades. I am as grateful to them now as I was when we published *Gulag: A History* in 2003. Many thanks to Nora Reichard, who has been my production editor for just about as long, as well as to managing editors Meredith Dros and Vimi Santokhi, production manager Bob Wojciechowski, designer Michael Collica, and the excellent publicists at Doubleday and Penguin, led by Sara Hayet and Annabel Huxley.

Notes

Preface to the paperback edition

xv In terms of high-end product influx into the US: https://www.businessinsider.com/donald-trump-jr-said-money-pouring-in-from-russia-2018-2

xv As of 2018, one out of every five condos: https://www.buzzfeednews.com/article/thomasfrank/secret-money-how-trump-made-millions-selling-condos-to

xv continued to buy into his businesses: https://www.usatoday.com/story/news/2018/01/10/trumps-secretive-real-estate-sales-continue-unabated/1018530001/

xv In the weeks after the election: https://thehill.com/policy/international/5035089-trump-organization-officially-launches-new-saudi-arabia-tower/

xv Trump's family also created a crypto currency business: https://www.reuters.com/business/finance/how-trump-family-took-over-crypto-firm-it-raised-hundreds-millions-2025-03-31/

xv Ominously, his administration did indeed: https://www.reuters.com/legal/us-sec-tron-founder-justin-sun-explore-resolution-civil-fraud-case-2025-02-26/

xv Justin Sun, a Chinese entrepreneur: Sun has denied the SEC charges: https://edition.cnn.com/2025/02/28/business/crypto-mogul-trump-coins-civil-fraud-charges/index.html; https://www.bbc.co.uk/news/articles/c4gzz5wdg410

xv American tech company CEOs: https://edition.cnn.com/2025/01/25/politics/trumps-foreign-business-partners-promoting-projects-invs/index.html

xvi Several lesser-known companies: https://www.notus.org/donald-trump/corporate-donations-trump-inauguration

xvi Soon afterwards, in a late-night purge: https://abcnews.go.com/Politics/trump-fires-17-independent-watchdogs-multiple-agencies-late/story?id=118097873

xvi slashed jobs at the National Highway Traffic Safety Administration: https://apnews.com/article/musk-trump-autonomous-selfdriving-doge-auto-safety-99b369c5e3ccd3e7c09b6951604b3a0a

xvi Musk oversaw mass firings: https://www.nytimes.com/2025/02/11/us/politics/elon-musk-companies-conflicts.html

xvi began using or considering the use of Starlink: https://www.nbcnews.com/tech/elon-musk/elon-musk-starlink-growing-footprint-federal-government-rcna195400

xvi the State Department planned to buy: https://www.nytimes.com/2025/02/12/us/politics/trump-tesla-musk-cybertruck.html?smid=url-share

xvii The Treasury Department announced: https://www.wsj.com/articles/trump-administration-curbs-enforcement-of-the-corporate-transparency-act-4ea50e81

xvii Trump ordered a full work stoppage: https://www.npr.org/2025/02/10/nx-s1-5292123/the-trump-administration-has-stopped-work-at-the-cfpb-heres-what-the-agency-does

xvii He also fired top officials: https://www.washingtonpost.com/politics/2025/02/13/trump-firings-watchdogs/

xvii proposing that Ukraine hand over half of its rare-mineral wealth: https://www.washingtonpost.com/politics/2025/02/15/ukraine-rejects-trump-administration-request-half-its-mineral-wealth/

xviii Among them were America's foreign broadcasters: https://x.com/elonmusk/status/1888574212316582230

Introduction: Autocracy, Inc.

2 the strongmen who lead: They are also sometimes called personalist dictators. See Erica Frantz, Andrea Kendall-Taylor, and Joe Wright,

The Origins of Elected Strongmen: How Personalist Parties Destroy Democracy from Within (Oxford: Oxford University Press, 2024).

3 perhaps three dozen others: Freedom House lists fifty-six countries as "Not Free" in *Freedom in the World,* 2024, freedomhouse.org, accessed Feb. 20, 2024.

3 Alexander Lukashenko's unpopular regime: "Belarus: Statement by the High Representative on Behalf of the European Union on the Third Anniversary of the Fraudulent Presidential Elections," European Neighbourhood Policy and Enlargement Negotiations (DG NEAR), Aug. 8, 2023, neighbourhood-enlargement.ec.europa.eu; OSCE, "OSCE Monitors Condemn Flawed Belarus Vote, Crackdown," press release, Dec. 20, 2010, www.oscepa.org.

3 modeled on a similar project in Suzhou: Ma Li Wenbo and Yekaterina Radionova, "The Great Stone China-Belarus Industrial Park," Dreams Come True, 2019, www.mofcom.gov.cn, accessed Feb. 16, 2024.

3 Iran and Belarus exchanged high-level diplomatic visits: Claudia Chiappa, "Lukashenko to Iran: Let's Be BFFs," *Politico,* Oct. 17, 2023.

4 Russia sent Russian journalists: "Belarus TV Staffs Up with Kremlin-Funded Journalists—RBC," *Moscow Times,* Sept. 1, 2020.

4 loans from Russia: "Russia Discusses Debt, Energy Stability with Venezuela," Reuters, Dec. 14, 2022.

4 A Belarusian company assembles tractors: "Venezuela Assembles Tractors with Support from Belarus," *Kawsachun News,* March 15, 2022.

4 illicit Venezuelan gold trade: "How Venezuela's Stolen Gold Ended Up in Turkey, Uganda, and Beyond," *InSight Crime,* March 21, 2019.

4 Chinese-made water cannons: "Venezuela Defends Purchase of Chinese Riot-Control Gear After More Than 70 Deaths in Street Protests," *South China Morning Post,* June 19, 2017.

4 Chinese-designed surveillance technology: Alessandra Soler and Giovana Fleck, "Is China Exporting Its Surveillance State to Venezuela?," Global Voices, Sept. 28, 2021, globalvoices.org.

4 dictators are widely despised: In mid-2020, only 13 percent of Venezuelans viewed Maduro positively. Also in 2020, just before the election, independent pollsters showed Lukashenko with 29.5 percent of public support.

4 Both would lose: Cynthia J. Arnson, ed., *Venezuela's Authoritarian Allies: The Ties That Bind?* (Washington, D.C.: Woodrow Wilson International Center for Scholars, 2021), 9, www.wilsoncenter.org.

6 When the Soviet premier: William Taubman, *Khrushchev: The Man and His Era* (New York: W. W. Norton, 2004), 553.

6 Even in the early part of this century: Sergei Guriev and Daniel Treisman have described this slicker form of autocracy in *Spin Dictators: The Changing Face of Tyranny in the 21st Century* (Princeton, N.J.: Princeton University Press, 2022).

7 The Iranian regime does not conceal: Raz Zimmt, "As President Raisi Visits China: Renewed Debate on Iran's Policy Regarding Uyghur Muslims," Lester and Sally Entin Faculty of Humanities, Tel Aviv University, March 2023, en-humanities.tau.ac.il.

7 "Maduro model": Interview with Srdja Popovic, Aug. 6, 2020.

8 Sometimes communists fought communists: The People's Republic of China, for example, fought the People's Republic of Vietnam.

8 "restricted, truncated, false": Lenin, *Collected Works,* vol. 28 (Moscow: Progress Publishers, 1965), 243.

8 "Only scoundrels and simpletons": Vladimir I. Lenin, "Greetings to Italian, French, and German Communists," Oct. 10, 1919, in *Collected Works,* 4th ed. (Moscow: Progress Publishers, 1965), 30:52–62, www.marxists.org.

8 Mussolini, the Italian leader: Jill Lepore, "The Last Time Democracy Almost Died," *The New Yorker,* Jan. 27, 2020.

8 He wrote in *Mein Kampf*: Rainer Zitelmann, *Hitler's National Socialism* (Oxford: Management Books, 2000, 2022).

9 As early as 1929: Mao Zedong, "On Correcting Mistaken Ideas in the Party," Dec. 1929, www.marxists.org.

9 "Burma's 'parliamentary democracy'": Revolutionary Council of the Union of Burma, "The Burmese Way to Socialism," April 1962, www.scribd.com.

9 "ideologically self-conscious, vanguard": Ladan Boroumand and Roya Boroumand, "Terror, Islam, and Democracy," *Journal of Democracy* 13, no. 2 (April 2002).

11 The document went on to instruct: Chris Buckley, "China Takes Aim at Western Ideas," *New York Times,* Aug. 19, 2013.

12 accusing the Russian opposition: Interfax-Ukraine, "Putin Calls 'Color Revolutions' an Instrument of Destabilization," *Kyiv Post,* Dec. 15, 2011.

13 They built torture chambers: Anne Applebaum and Nataliya Gumenyuk, "Incompetence and Torture in Occupied Ukraine," *Atlantic,* Feb. 14, 2023, www.theatlantic.com.

13 They kidnapped thousands of children: "Russia's Systematic Program for the Re-education and Adoption of Ukraine's Children," Conflict Observatory, Feb. 14, 2023, hub.conflictobservatory.org.

13 They deliberately targeted emergency workers: Rikard Jozwiak, "Ukraine Accuses Russia of Targeting Rescue Workers in Deadly Strike," RFE/RL, Aug. 8, 2023, www.rferl.org.

14 making a mockery: Maria Domańska, Iwona Wiśniewska, and Piotr Żochowski, "Caught in the Jaws of the 'Russkiy Mir': Ukraine's Occupied Regions a Year After Their Annexation," *Ośrodek Studiów Wschodnich* (Warsaw), Oct. 11, 2023, www.osw.waw.pl.

14 "This is not about Ukraine": Sergei Lavrov, "Lavrov Said That There Is Hope for a Compromise in Negotiations with Ukraine," Tass, March 16, 2022, tass.ru.

15 "Would we stand up": Joe Biden, "Remarks by President Biden Ahead of the One-Year Anniversary of Russia's Brutal and Unprovoked Invasion of Ukraine," White House, Feb. 21, 2023, www.whitehouse.gov.

16 "interference in the internal affairs": "Joint Statement of the Russian Federation and the People's Republic of China on the International Relations Entering a New Era and the Global Sustainable Development," President of Russia, Feb. 4, 2022, www.en.kremlin.ru.

16 Instead, they profited: Dan De Luce, "China Helps Russia Evade Sanctions, Likely Supplies Moscow with War Tech Used in Ukraine," NBC News, July 27, 2023, www.nbcnews.com.

16 Iran exported thousands of lethal drones: Armani Syed, "Iranian 'Kamikaze' Drones: Why Russia Uses Them in Ukraine," *Time,* Oct. 20, 2022, time.com.

16 North Korea supplied ammunition: Mike Eckel, "Report: North Korea Shipping Ammunition, Weaponry 'at Scale' to Russia," RFE/RL, Oct. 17, 2023, www.rferl.org.

16 Belarus allowed Russian troops: Oleksiy Pavlysh, *Ukrainska Pravda,* July 18, 2022, as reported in www.yahoo.com.

16 Turkey, Georgia, Kyrgyzstan, and Kazakhstan: Alexander Kupatadze and Erica Marat, *Under the Radar: How Russia Outmanoeuvres Western Sanctions with Help from Its Neighbours,* Serious Organised Crime & Anti-Corruption Evidence Research Programme, Aug. 2023.

17 A leaked document: Catherine Belton, "Russia Oozes Confidence as It Promotes Anti-Western Global Alliances," *Washington Post,* Jan. 27, 2024.

1 *The Greed That Binds*

19 In the summer of 1967: Thane Gustafson, *The Bridge: Natural Gas in a Redivided Europe* (Cambridge, Mass.: Harvard University Press, 2020), 40.

20 the first gas pipelines: "Bonn and Moscow Sign Pact Trading Pipes for Gas," *New York Times,* Feb. 2, 1970.

20 His reasoning was mostly political: Per Högselius, *Red Gas: Russia and the Origins of European Energy Dependence* (New York: Palgrave Macmillan, 2013), 118–19.

21 famous speech in 1963: Egon Bahr, "Wandel durch Annäherung," speech in the Evangelical Academy Tutzing, July 15, 1963, 100(0) Schlüsseldokumente zur deutschen Geschichte im 20. Jahrhundert, 100(0) Schlüsseldokumente zur russischen und sowjetischen Geschichte (1917–1991), Bayerische Staatsbibliothek, Munich, www.1000dokumente.de.

21 West Germany frequently paid: Monica Raymunt, "West Germany's Cold War Ransoming of Prisoners Encouraged Fraud: Research," Reuters, April 10, 2014.

21 "emotive imprecision": Timothy Garton Ash, *In Europe's Name: Germany and the Divided Continent* (New York: Vintage Press, 1994).

21 "to detach Germany from NATO": Charles W. Carter, "The Evolution of US Policy Toward West German–Soviet Trade Relations, 1969–89," *International History Review* 34, no. 2 (June 2012): 223.

22 "idealistic preacher": Ibid., 229.

22 Caspar Weinberger, worried out loud: Ibid., 221–44.

25 A more liberal China: Julian Gewirtz, *Unlikely Partners: Chinese Reformers, Western Economists, and the Making of Global China* (Cambridge, Mass.: Harvard University Press, 2017).

25 "there's much to be gained": Ronald Reagan, "Remarks upon Return-

ing from China," May 1, 1984, Ronald Reagan Presidential Library, www.reaganlibrary.gov.

26 "growing interdependence would": Bill Clinton, "President Clinton's Remarks on China," Clinton White House, Oct. 24, 1997, clintonwhitehouse4.archives.gov.

26 "I believe the choice": Bill Clinton, "Full Text of Clinton's Speech on China Trade Bill," Institute for Agriculture and Trade Policy, March 8, 2000, www.iatp.org.

26 "Why We Need Beijing": Gerhard Schröder, "China: Warum wir Peking brauchen," *Die Zeit,* July 17, 2008, www.zeit.de.

27 Britain was "delusional": Rhyannon Bartlett, Pak Yiu, and staff writers, "Britain 'Delusional' over Chinese Democracy: Ex-Gov. Patten," *Nikkei Asia,* July 1, 2022, asia.nikkei.com.

28 *Izvestiya:* Leon Aron, *Roads to the Temple: Truth, Memory, Ideas and Ideals in the Making of the Russian Revolution, 1987–1991* (New Haven, Conn.: Yale University Press, 2012), 37 and 49.

28 nine out of ten people said: Leon Aron, *Roads to the Temple: Truth, Memory, Ideas, and Ideals in the Making of the Russian Revolution, 1987–1991* (New Haven, Conn.: Yale University Press, 2012), 30.

28 "I was absolutely sure": Yegor Gaidar, "Conversations with History: Yegor Gaidar," YouTube, 2008.

29 "really recruited me": Catherine Belton, *Putin's People: How the KGB Took Back Russia and Then Took On the West* (New York: Farrar, Straus and Giroux, 2020), 21–23.

29 "an inchoate democratic system": Karen Dawisha, *Putin's Kleptocracy: Who Owns Russia?* (New York: Simon & Schuster, 2015), 8.

30 The first glimmer of the idea: Belton, *Putin's People,* 19–49.

31 The goods were indeed sold: Dawisha, *Putin's Kleptocracy,* 106–32; Belton, *Putin's People,* 87–91.

32 No charges against Putin: Dawisha, *Putin's Kleptocracy,* 132–45.

32 Allegedly: Dawisha, *Putin's Kleptocracy,* 140.

33 "only a democratic state is capable": Vladimir Putin, "Послание Президента Российской Федерации от 08.07.2000 г. б/н," Президент России, July 7, 2000, www.kremlin.ru.

33 "rule of law, free elections": Vladimir Putin, "Послание Президента

Российской Федерации от 18.04.2002," Kremlin.ru, April 18, 2002, www.kremlin.ru.

35 "Crime and corruption": Anne Applebaum, "Should Putin Host the G-8?," *The Spectator,* July 8, 2006.

35 "process of democratization": "G-8 Leaders Issue Statement on Energy," Voice of America, July 13, 2006, voanews.com.

36 "Cavernous holes gouge": Casey Michel, *American Kleptocracy* (New York: St. Martin's Press, 2021), 206.

37 Kolomoisky bought the mill: "United States Files Civil Forfeiture Complaint for Proceeds of Alleged Fraud and Theft from PrivatBank in Ukraine," Department of Justice, Jan. 20, 2022, www.justice.gov.

37 American real estate agents: Craig Unger, "Trump's Businesses Are Full of Dirty Russian Money. The Scandal Is That It's Legal," *Washington Post,* March 29, 2019.

37 One in five condos: Dan Alexander, "Mysterious Buyer Pumps $2.9 Million into President Trump's Coffers," *Forbes,* March 19, 2019, www.forbes.com.

38 fighting the nationalization of PrivatBank: Gabriel Gavin, "Ukraine Launches Criminal Case Against Oligarch Kolomoisky," *Politico,* Sept. 2, 2023, www.politico.eu.

11 *Kleptocracy Metastasizes*

44 Venezuela's Supreme Court quashed: Agustín Blanco Muñoz, *Habla Jesús Urdaneta Hernandez, el comandante irreductible* (Caracas: Universidad Central de Venezuela, 2003), 28.

45 During the fourteen years Chávez held power: "Los billonarios recursos que Pdvsa logró . . . y perdió," Transparencia Venezuela, May 2020, transparenciave.org. According to Transparencia Venezuela, part of Transparency International, the total value of oil produced was nearer $1.2 trillion, but $400 billion of that was used for internal consumptions at near-zero prices.

45 Banco Espírito Santo: "Portugal Investigating Fraud Linked to Venezuela PDVSA Funds, PDVSA Says," Reuters, June 24, 2017.

45 Swiss banks were hiding $10 billion: Sylvain Besson and Christian Brönnimann, "Une nouvelle enquête vise les milliards de la corruption vénézuélienne," *Tribune de Genève,* Jan. 16, 2021, www.tdg.ch.

46 banks in the principality of Andorra: Valentina Lares and Nathan Jaccard, "Los dineros negros de Andorra se lavan en el Caribe," Armando Info, Dec. 1, 2021, armando.info.

46 127 cases of large-scale corruption: "Los billonarios recursos que Pdvsa logró . . . y perdió."

46 "democratization of kleptocracy": Conversation with Francisco Toro, autumn 2023.

47 the total amount stolen before 2013: Lucas Goyret, "Corrupción chavista: Cuál es el destino de los miles de millones de dólares robados por la dictadura venezolana que son decomisados por Estados Unidos," *Infobae,* June 5, 2021, www.infobae.com.

47 a Miami court has charged: Federico Parra, "Venezuelan Officials, Others Charged with Laundering $1.2 Billion in Oil Funds," *Miami Herald,* July 25, 2018.

47 Investigations into that case: Jay Weaver and Antonio M. Delgado, "Venezuela's Elite Face Scrutiny in $1.2 Billion Laundering Probe," *Miami Herald,* Nov. 3, 2019.

48 Jeremy Corbyn: "British Opposition Leader Corbyn Declines to Condemn Venezuela's Maduro," Reuters, Aug. 7, 2017.

48 The first blow came in 2002–3: Robert Rapier, "How Venezuela Ruined Its Oil Industry," *Forbes,* May 7, 2017, www.forbes.com.

50 suspected and indeed convicted of smuggling cocaine: Alfredo Meza, "Corrupt Military Officials Helping Venezuela Drug Trade Flourish," *El País,* Sept. 26, 2013, english.elpais.com.

50 illegal and unregulated gold mines: Jose Guarnizo, "On the Border of Colombia and Venezuela, Illegal Gold Mining Unites Armed Forces," *Mongabay,* May 12, 2023, news.mongabay.com.

51 Chinese-backed high-speed railway: Alexander Olvera, "Para pastorear vacas quedó ferrocarril Tinaco-Anaco," El Pitazo, 2016, www.youtube.com.

52 "They sometimes call us": Imdat Oner, *Turkey and Venezuela: An Alliance of Convenience* (Washington, D.C.: Wilson Center, 2020), www.wilsoncenter.org.

53 launder money: Joseph M. Humire, "The Maduro-Hezbollah Nexus: How Iran-Backed Networks Prop Up the Venezuelan Regime," The Atlantic Council, Oct. 7, 2020, atlanticcouncil.org.

54 high-tech components from U.S. companies: "22-CR-434," Department of Justice, Oct. 19, 2022, www.justice.gov.

54 "the man Presidents around the world": Uebert Angel, TheMillionaireAcademy, 2023, themillionaireacademy.org.

55 four-part Al Jazeera documentary: Al Jazeera Investigations, *Gold Mafia*, youtube.com.

55 Through a spokesman: "Uebert Angel's Office Responds to Al-Jazeera Documentary, *The Zimbabwean,* March 25, 2023," www.thezimbabwean.co.

55 Angel's personal assistant: Rikki Doolan (@realrikkidoolan), X.com, 2023, twitter.com/realrikkidoolan.

56 In a video: "Pastor Rikki Doolan Responds on Gold Mafia Aljazeera Documentary," www.youtube.com/watch?v=hblbCh8xi4s.

57 He and Mnangagwa: MacDonald Dzirutwe, "Ghosts of Past Massacres Haunt Zimbabwe's Mnangagwa Before Election," July 6, 2018, Reuters. Mnangagwa denies these charges.

58 launder or accept criminal or stolen wealth: Lily Sabol, "Kleptocratic Adaptation: Anticipating the Next Stage in the Battle Against Transnational Kleptocracy," National Endowment for Democracy, Jan. 17, 2023, www.ned.org.

58 Turkish schemes to transport gold: Mark Lowen, "Turkey Warned over Venezuela Gold Trade," BBC, Feb. 2, 2019, www.bbc.com/news.

59 neither of which had previously exported wood: Rikard Jozwiak, Kubatbek Aibashov, and Chris Rickleton, "Reexports to Russia: How the Ukraine War Made Trade Boom in Kyrgyzstan," RFE/RL, Feb. 18, 2023, www.rferl.org.

59 permitted a relatively free press: "Joint Statement After Kyrgyz's Recent Crackdowns on Independent Media," Civil Rights Defenders, Jan. 16, 2024, crd.org.

59 Bektour Iskender: Bektour Iskender, "The Crime-Fighting Power of Cross-Border Investigative Journalism," TED, April 2022, ted.com.

60 Kyrgyzstan had blocked the Kloop websites: RFE/RL's Kyrgyz Service, "Kyrgyzstan Blocks Independent Kloop Website's Kyrgyz Segment," RFE/RL, Nov. 10, 2023, www.rferl.org.

60 The Zimbabwe Human Rights Forum documented: Zimbabwe

Human Rights Forum, "Political Violence Report 2008," Feb. 13, 2009, 2, ntjwg.uwazi.io.

61 amending the constitution in 2021: Kitsepile Nyathi, "Zimbabwe's Mnangagwa Entrenching His Power with Constitution Changes," *Citizen,* April 10, 2021, www.thecitizen.co.tz.

61 distributed bribes, disguised as housing loans: Albert Mpofu, "Controversy Erupts over Housing Loans to Judges Before Elections in Zimbabwe," Change Radio Zimbabwe, June 9, 2023, changeradiozimbabwe.com.

61 the "Patriotic Bill": "Zimbabwe: Parliament's Passing of 'Patriotic Bill' Is a Grave Assault on the Human Rights," Amnesty International, June 9, 2023, www.amnesty.org.

62 more U.S. and EU sanctions: "Treasury Takes Additional Actions in Zimbabwe," U.S. Treasury Department, Dec. 12, 2022, home .treasury.gov.

62 The Chinese had provided weapons: Olayiwola Abegunrin and Charity Manyeruke, *China's Power in Africa: A New Global Order* (London: Palgrave Macmillan, 2020).

62 a million doses of its Sinovac COVID-19 vaccine: Guo Shaochun, "Promoting China-Zimbabwe Ties to a New Height," Embassy of the People's Republic of China in the Republic of Zimbabwe, Oct. 2, 2022, zw.china-embassy.gov.cn.

62 processing facilities for lithium: Columbus Mavhunga, "Zimbabwe, Chinese Investors Sign $2.8B Metals Park Deal," VOA News, Sept. 22, 2022, www.voanews.com.

62 Zimbabwe got broadband deals: "Zimbabwe Turns to Chinese Technology to Expand Surveillance of Citizens," *Africa Defense Forum,* Jan. 17, 2023, adf-magazine.com.

63 "law enforcement purposes": Allen Munoriyarwa, "Video Surveillance in Southern Africa," Media Policy and Democracy Project, May 7, 2020, www.mediaanddemocracy.com.

63 a platinum-mining concession: Henry Foy, Nastassia Astrasheuskaya, and David Pilling, "Russia: Vladimir Putin's Pivot to Africa," *Financial Times,* Jan. 21, 2019, www.ft.com.

63 Putin welcomed Mnangagwa to Moscow: Brian Latham et al.,

"Mnangagwa Seeks Cash in Russia as Zimbabwe Slides into Chaos," Bloomberg.com, Jan. 15, 2019.

63 Russian investment in Zimbabwe's diamond industry: Bloomberg, "Russian Diamond Giant Alrosa Is Returning to Zimbabwe," *Moscow Times,* Jan. 15, 2019.

63 "This bird will soon be gracing our skies": Nick Mangwana (@nickmangwana), Twitter, July 27, 2023, 10:23 a.m., x.com/nickmangwana.

III *Controlling the Narrative*

66 "Vladimir Putin may yet make her a prophet": Max Frankel, review of *Iron Curtain,* by Anne Applebaum, *New York Times,* Nov. 21, 2012, www.nytimes.com. Frankel's review was negative, largely because he thought the Soviet tactics used in the book were old news and could never be brought back. Two years later, in 2014, the Russian occupations of Crimea and eastern Ukraine followed almost exactly the same playbook that the Red Army and NKVD had used in 1945.

67 prohibited an extraordinarily wide range of content: Jason P. Abbott, "Of Grass Mud Horses and Rice Bunnies: Chinese Internet Users Challenge Beijing's Censorship and Internet Controls," *Asian Politics and Policy* 11, no. 1 (2019): 162–77; Peng Li, "Provisional Management Regulations for the International Connection of Computer Information Networks of the People's Republic of China," Feb. 1, 1996, DigiChina, digichina.stanford.edu.

67 Yahoo agreed to sign: Jim Hu, "Yahoo Yields to Chinese Web Laws," CNET, Aug. 14, 2002, cnet.com.

68 police departments of at least thirty-one provinces: Anne Applebaum, "Let a Thousand Filters Bloom," *Washington Post,* July 19, 2005.

68 Google struggled to adhere: Kaveh Waddell, "Why Google Quit China—and Why It's Heading Back," *Atlantic,* Jan. 19, 2016, www.theatlantic.com.

68 The company later worked secretly: Ryan Gallagher, "Google Plans to Launch Censored Search Engine in China, Leaked Documents Reveal," *Intercept,* Aug. 1, 2018, theintercept.com; "Google's Project Dragonfly 'Terminated' in China," BBC, July 17, 2019, www.bbc.com.

69 Voice-recognition technology and even DNA swabs: Ross Ander-

sen, "China's Artificial Intelligence Surveillance State Goes Global," *Atlantic,* Sept. 15, 2020, www.theatlantic.com.

69 "Chinese algorithms will be able": Ibid.

70 surveillance, and AI systems: Sheena Chestnut Greitens, "Dealing with Demand for China's Global Surveillance Exports," Brookings Institution, April 2020, www.brookings.edu.

70 every lamppost in the city-state: Steven Feldstein, "How Artificial Intelligence Is Reshaping Repression," *Journal of Democracy* 30, no. 1 (Jan. 2019).

70 President Mnangagwa bought: Problem Masau, "Smart Anti-Crime Solutions," ChinAfrica, May 3, 2024, chinafrica.cn.

72 "bring other countries' models": Ibid.

72 emphasizing one line of the lyrics: Lun Tian Yew, "Protests Erupt in Xinjiang and Beijing After Deadly Fire," Reuters, Nov. 26, 2022.

74 The North Koreans, famously, hold: Josh Smith, "Inside the Spectacle and Symbolism of North Korea's Mass Games," Reuters, Sept. 6, 2018.

74 Chinese media mocked the laxity of the American response: Julie Nolke, "Covid-19—Once upon a Virus . . . ," YouTube, 2020, www.youtube.com.

74 "Seeing such scenarios": "Chinese Netizens Jeer Riot in US Capitol as 'Karma,' Say Bubbles of 'Democracy and Freedom' Have Burst," *Global Times,* Jan. 7, 2021, globaltimes.cn.

75 "Foreign hostile forces have": Brett McKeehan, "China's Propaganda Machine Is Intensifying Its 'People's War' to Catch American Spies," CNN, Oct. 18, 2021, www.cnn.com.

75 an average of eighteen times a day: Nataliya Popovych et al., "Image of European Countries on Russian TV," Ukraine Crisis Media Center, May 2018, uacrisis.org.

75 an alarmingly intimate acquaintance: Pjotr Sauer, "Russia Outlaws 'International LGBT Public Movement' as Extremist," *Guardian,* Nov. 30, 2023.

76 Putin's way of building alliances: Documentation in Kristina Stoeckl and Dmitry Uzlaner, *The Moralist International: Russia in the Global Cultural Wars* (New York: Fordham University Press, 2022).

76 in the name of Islamic purity: Anne Applebaum, "Conservatives

and the False Romance of Russia," *Atlantic,* Dec. 12, 2019, www.theatlantic.com.

76 The Russian state harasses and represses: Kate Shellnutt, "Russian Evangelicals Penalized Most Under Anti-Evangelism Law," *Christianity Today,* May 7, 2019, www.christianitytoday.com.

76 "Russia is our friend": David Neiwert, "When White Nationalists Chant Their Weird Slogans, What Do They Mean?," Southern Poverty Law Center, Oct. 10, 2017, www.splcenter.org.

76 covertly funding some of them: Elizabeth G. Arsenault and Joseph Stabile, "Confronting Russia's Role in Transnational White Supremacist Extremism," Just Security, Feb. 6, 2020, www.justsecurity.org.

77 the Russian state banned: Sauer, "Russia Outlaws 'International LGBT Public Movement' as Extremist"; Darya Tarasova, Gul Tuysuz, and Jen Deaton, "Police Raid Gay Venues in Russia After Top Court Bans 'International LGBTQ Movement,'" CNN, Dec. 4, 2023, edition.cnn.com.

77 "Outsiders cannot dictate to us": Sabiti Makara and Vibeke Wang, "Uganda: A Story of Persistent Autocratic Rule," in *Democratic Backsliding in Africa?: Autocratization, Resilience, and Contention,* ed. Leonardo R. Arriola, Lise Rakner, and Nicolas Van de Walle (Oxford: Oxford University Press, 2022).

77 Orbán's deep financial and political ties: Anne Applebaum, "Tucker Carlson, the American Face of Authoritarian Propaganda," *Atlantic,* Sept. 21, 2023, www.theatlantic.com.

77 Sometimes he invited celebrities: Peter Pomerantsev, "Beyond Propaganda," *Foreign Policy,* June 23, 2015, foreignpolicy.com.

78 an excellent tourist destination: Annia Ciezadlo, "Analysis: Why Assad's Propaganda Isn't as Crazy as It Seems," Atlantic Council, Oct. 7, 2016, www.atlanticcouncil.org.

80 coined the term "sharp power": Christopher Walker, "What Is 'Sharp Power'?," *Journal of Democracy* 29, no. 3 (July 2018), www.journalofdemocracy.org.

80 Many are coordinated by the United Front: Didi Kirsten Tatlow, "China's Influence Efforts in Germany Involve Students," *Atlantic,* July 12, 2019, www.theatlantic.com.

81 Confucius Institutes flourish: "Confucius Institute," Confucius Institute, 2024, accessed Feb. 18, 2024, ci.cn; Wagdy Sawahel, "Confucius Institutes Increase as Another Opens in Djibouti," *University World News,* April 6, 2023.

81 Their news: Joshua Kurlantzick, *Beijing's Global Media Offensive: China's Uneven Campaign to Influence Asia and the World* (Oxford: Oxford University Press, 2023), 181–99.

81 not many people watch: Joshua Kurlantzick, "Can China's State Media Become as Trusted as the BBC?," *Foreign Policy,* Dec. 5, 2022, foreignpolicy.com.

82 dialogue and commentary all translated: Joshua Eisenman, "China's Media Propaganda in Africa: A Strategic Assessment," United States Institute of Peace, March 16, 2023, www.usip.org.

82 The Chinese Communist Party uses student associations: Ryan Fedasiuk, "How China's United Front System Works Overseas," *Strategist,* April 13, 2022, www.aspistrategist.org.au.

82 "borrowing boats to reach the sea": Eisenman, "China's Media Propaganda in Africa."

83 lifted directly from the Xinhua wire: "Russia Has No Expansionist Plans in Europe: Lavrov," Telesur English, Nov. 27, 2023, www.telesurenglish.net.

83 One March 2020 headline: "Informe: El nuevo coronavirus es resultado de un complot sionista," HispanTV, March 19, 2020, www.hispantv.com.

83 RT—Russia Today—has a bigger profile: Martina Schwikowski, "Russia Targets Africa with Propaganda Machine," DW, Nov. 29, 2022, www.dw.com.

84 RT appears to be welcome now in Algiers: "RT Moves Its Pawns in Africa, Opening a Bureau in Algeria," Reporters Without Borders, April 4, 2023, rsf.org.

84 A South African headquarters: Thinus Ferreira, "Russia's RT Channel Eyes African Expansion with SA Headquarters," News24, July 26, 2022, www.news24.com.

84 The true purpose of RT: Katie Zabadski, "Putin's Propaganda TV Lies About Its Popularity," *Daily Beast,* April 14, 2017. A 2015 cache

of documents dumped by disgruntled old RIA Novosti employees on *The Daily Beast* suggest at that point RT was being watched by fewer than thirty thousand U.S. households on any given night; its most successful market then appeared to be the U.K., where it attracted "0.17 percent of the total viewing population."

84 They manufactured anti-Muslim hysteria: Mobashra Tazamal, "How Russian Bots Instrumentalized Islamophobia (but Don't Just Blame the Bots)," Bridge Initiative, Feb. 2, 2018, bridge.georgetown.edu.

84 a Facebook group called Secured Borders: NBC News, "How Russia Sent a Small Idaho Town into a Fake News Tailspin: NBC Left Field | After Truth," YouTube, www.youtube.com.

85 Spokesmen for the Russian Defense: Adan Salazar, "Russian Strikes Targeting US-Run Bio-Labs in Ukraine?," Infowars, Feb. 24, 2022, www.infowars.com.

85 Even after the suspension of the account: Justin Ling, "How a QAnon Conspiracy Theory About Ukraine Bioweapons Became Mainstream Disinformation," CBC, April 13, 2022, www.cbc.ca.

86 "stop lying and telling us what's going on here": "Tucker: The Pentagon Is Lying About Bio Labs in Ukraine," Fox News, March 9, 2022, www.foxnews.com.

86 Chinese Foreign Ministry spokesman: "Foreign Ministry Spokesperson Zhao Lijian's Regular Press Conference on March 8, 2022," Ministry of Foreign Affairs of the People's Republic of China, March 9, 2022, fmprc.gov.cn.

86 Xinhua ran multiple headlines: "U.S.-Led Biolabs Pose Potential Threats to People of Ukraine and Beyond: Ukrainian Ex-officer," Xinhua, April 14, 2022, english.news.cn; "Russia Urges U.S. to Explain Purpose of Biological Labs in Ukraine," Xinhua, March 10, 2022, english.news.cn.

86 U.S. diplomats vociferously contradicted: Edward Wong, "U.S. Fights Bioweapons Disinformation Pushed by Russia and China," *New York Times,* March 10, 2022.

86 So did Telesur: Jose C. Rodriguez, "US Resumes Biolab Program in Ukraine," Telesur English, April 7, 2023, www.telesurenglish.net.

86 PressTV, and the various: "Russia Says Has Documents Showing US Biolab Activities in Ukraine," PressTV, Jan. 31, 2023, www.presstv.ir.

87 a quarter of Americans believed: Ling, "How a QAnon Conspiracy Theory About Ukraine Bioweapons Became Mainstream Disinformation."

88 But according to the U.S. State Department's Global Engagement Center: U.S. Department of State, "The Kremlin's Efforts to Covertly Spread Disinformation in Latin America," press release, Nov. 7, 2023, www.state.gov; María Zakharova, "BioBiden," Pressenza International Press Agency, March 29, 2022, www.pressenza.com.

88 a long, straight-faced official statement: Julian Borger, Jennifer Rankin, and Martin Farrer, "Russia Makes Claims of US-Backed Biological Weapon Plot at UN," *Guardian,* March 11, 2022.

89 Although the company: Hannah Gelbart, "The UK Company Spreading Russian Fake News to Millions," BBC, April 4, 2023, www.bbc.com/news.

90 African Initiative: Michael R. Gordon et al., "Russian Intelligence Is Pushing False Claims of U.S. Biological Testing in Africa, U.S. Says," *Wall Street Journal,* Feb. 8, 2024.

91 When someone is quickly scrolling: Viginum, "RRN: A Complex and Persistent Information Manipulation Campaign," General Secretariat for Defense and National Security, République Française, July 19, 2023, www.sgdsn.gouv.fr.

91 Doppelganger's efforts: Ibid.

91 In the autumn of 2023: Catherine Belton and Joseph Menn, "Russian Trolls Target U.S. Support for Ukraine, Kremlin Documents Show," *Washington Post,* April 8, 2024.

92 "We see directly": Avery Lotz, "House Intelligence Committee Chair Says Russian Propaganda Has Spread Through Parts of GOP," CNN, April 7, 2024, cnn.com.

93 At its peak, the angry coverage: Oiwan Lam, "Amidst Typhoon Rescue Efforts in Japan, a Taiwanese Diplomat Dies. Did Misinformation Play a Role?," Global Voices, Sept. 22, 2018, globalvoices.org.

94 devastating wildfire in Maui: Steven L. Myers, "China Sows Disinformation About Hawaii Fires Using New Techniques," *New York Times,* Sept. 11, 2023.

94 In the spring of 2024: Tiffany Hsu and Steven L. Myers, "China's Advancing Efforts to Influence the U.S. Election Raise Alarms,"

New York Times, April 1, 2024; Elise Thomas, "Pro-CCP Spamouflage Campaign Experiments with New Tactics Targeting the US," *Digital Dispatches,* Institute for Strategic Dialogue, April 1, 2024, www.isdglobal.org/.

95 Notable were two kinds of messages: López Obrador, a left-wing leader with a strong autocratic streak, put together his own much more powerful combination of highly partisan media and social media bots, using the latter to bombard followers with the former. The Venezuelan accounts did the same, but using material from Telesur, HispanTV, and RT Actualidad. Nearly two-thirds of accounts that frequently share material from RT Actualidad in Mexico were likely to share material promoting López Obrador as well.

95 Venezuela-based and pro-Russian trolls: Javier Lesaca, "Russian Network Used Venezuelan Accounts to Deepen Catalan Crisis," *El País,* Nov. 11, 2017, english.elpais.com.

96 López Obrador handed over: Ryan C. Berg and Emiliano Polo, "The Political Implications of Mexico's New Militarism," *CSIS,* Sept. 5, 2023, www.csis.org.

96 He also promoted Russian narratives: Juan A. Quintanilla, "Letter to the Secretary of Foreign Affairs Marcelo Ebrard," Human Rights Watch, March 3, 2023, www.hrw.org.

96 A few months later: José Bautista and Michael Schwirtz, "Married Kremlin Spies, a Shadowy Mission to Moscow, and Unrest in Catalonia," *New York Times,* Sept. 23, 2021.

IV *Changing the Operating System*

99 "recognition of the inherent dignity": "Universal Declaration of Human Rights," UN.org.

99 "will promote and encourage": Helsinki Final Act, Conference on Security and Co-operation in Europe, OSCE, Aug. 1, 1975, www.osce.org.

100 "representative democracy": "Charter of the Organization of American States," cidh.oas.org.

100 "patchwork of false information": Ken Moritsugu and Jamey Keaten, "To China's Fury, UN Accuses Beijing of Uyghur Rights Abuses," AP News, Sept. 1, 2022, apnews.com.

101 the Russian president risks arrest: "Situation in Ukraine: ICC Judges Issue Arrest Warrants Against Vladimir Vladimirovich Putin and Maria Alekseyevna Lvova-Belova," International Criminal Court, March 17, 2023, www.icc-cpi.int.

101 At a Communist Party congress: "Full Text of Xi Jinping's Report at 19th CPC National Congress," *China Daily,* Nov. 4, 2017, chinadaily.com.cn.

101 "For the CCP to attain": Andréa Worden, "China at the UN Human Rights Council: Conjuring a 'Community of Shared Future for Humankind'?," in *An Emerging China-Centric Order: China's Vision for a New World Order in Practice,* ed. Nadège Rolland, National Bureau of Asian Research, NBR Special Report 87, Aug. 2020, www.nbr.org.

102 "There are not many countries": RG.RU, "О чем рассказал Владимир Путин на пленарном заседании ПМЭФ," Российская газета, June 2, 2017, rg.ru.

103 "We are moving towards a multipolar world": António Guterres, Instagram, Aug. 31, 2023, www.instagram.com.

104 the journalist Fareed Zakaria: Fareed Zakaria, *The Post-American World and the Rise of the Rest* (London: Penguin Books, 2008).

104 In service of this idea: Ivan U. Klyszcz, "Messianic Multipolarity: Russia's Resurrected Africa Doctrine," Riddle, April 6, 2023, ridl.io.

104 claimed he was protecting Russia: Mark Trevelyan, "As He Seizes Ukrainian Lands, Putin Is Silent on War Failings," Reuters, Sept. 30, 2022.

104 "We are now fighting": "Путин заявил, что Россия находится в авангарде создания справедливого мироустройства," Tass, Nov. 28, 2023, tass.ru.

104 a military dictatorship in power: "Mali: New Atrocities by Malian Army, Apparent Wagner Fighters," Human Rights Watch, July 24, 2023, www.hrw.org.

105 Mali Actu, a pro-Russian website: Mamadou Makadji, "L'Afrique revendique un monde multipolaire lors de la Semaine Russe de l'Énergie," Mali Actu, Oct. 15, 2023, maliactu.net.

105 "the aggressive emergence of the multipolar world": "Xinhua Commentary: This Time for Africa and a Multipolar World," Xinhua, Sept. 11, 2023, english.news.cn.

105 "China's diplomacy injects vitality": Danny Haiphong, "China's

Diplomacy Injects Vitality into the Multipolar World," CGTN, Sept. 27, 2023, news.cgtn.com.

105 "the multipolar, pluricentric world": Ben Norton, "Venezuela at UN: We Must Build Multipolar 'World Without Imperialism,'" Geopolitical Economy Report, Sept. 22, 2021, geopoliticaleconomy.com.

105 "strengthen ties of cooperation": Nicolás Maduro, Twitter, Aug. 8, 2023, x.com/NicolasMaduro.

105 "to establish a 'new multi-polarized'": Kim Tong, "North Korea Stresses Alignment with Russia Against US and Says Putin Could Visit at an Early Date," AP News, Jan. 21, 2024, apnews.com.

106 "stand against imperialism": Maziar Motamedi, "Iran's Raisi After 'Strategic' Ties in South America Tour," Al Jazeera, June 12, 2023, www.aljazeera.com.

108 Protasevich was one of the original editors: Anne Applebaum, "The 22-Year-Old Blogger Behind Protests in Belarus," *Atlantic,* Aug. 21, 2020, www.theatlantic.com.

108 declared him a "terrorist": Ivan Nechepurenko and Neil Vigdor, "Who Is Roman Protasevich, the Captive Journalist in Belarus?," *New York Times,* June 14, 2021.

108 "I am facing the death penalty": Chas Danner, Matt Stieb, and Eve Peyser, "European Union Bans Its Airlines from Flying over Belarus," *New York,* May 24, 2021, nymag.com.

108 the state did not kill him: Michelle Bachelet, "Belarus: 'You Are Not Human Beings,'" Amnesty International, Jan. 18, 2021, eurasia.amnesty.org.

108 a grotesque televised confession: Andrew Higgins, "With Pardon of Roman Protasevich, Belarus Fuels a Tale of Betrayal," *New York Times,* May 23, 2023.

109 "envy": Alexey Kovalev (@Alexey__Kovalev), Twitter, May 23, 2021, 9:56 a.m., twitter.com/Alexey__Kovalev.

109 "feasible and necessary": "Russia Defends Belarus over Plane Diversion," *Moscow Times,* May 24, 2021.

109 Freedom House calls this practice: "Transnational Repression: Understanding and Responding to Global Authoritarian Reach," Freedom House, 2024, accessed Feb. 18, 2024, freedomhouse.org/report/transnational-repression.

109 Another assassin, sent by the Russian state: Vanessa Guinan, "Rus-

sian Vadim Krasikov Convicted of Assassinating Chechen Tornike Khangoshvili in Tiergarten," *Washington Post,* Dec. 15, 2021.

109 falling down flights of stairs: Paul Kirby, "Russian Sausage Tycoon Pavel Antov Dies in Indian Hotel Fall," BBC, Dec. 27, 2022, www.bbc.com/news.

109 the south of France: Amit Chaturvedi, "Russian Businessman Dmitry Zelenov Dies Under Mysterious Circumstances," NDTV, Dec. 19, 2022, www.ndtv.com.

109 and Washington, D.C.: Michael Schaffer, "A Putin Critic Fell from a Building in Washington. Was It Really a Suicide?," *Politico,* Aug. 26, 2022.

109 killed or tried to kill Iranian exiles: Matthew Levitt, "Trends in Iranian External Assassination, Surveillance, and Abduction Plots," Combating Terrorism Center at West Point, Feb. 8, 2022, ctc.westpoint.edu.

110 to murder Masih Alinejad: "U.S. Attorney Announces Charges and New Arrest in Connection with Assassination Plot Directed from Iran," Department of Justice, Feb. 27, 2023, www.justice.gov.

110 "When you stand against China": Joanna Kakissis, "Uighurs in Turkey Fear China's Long Arm Has Reached Their Place of Refuge," NPR, March 13, 2020, www.npr.org.

110 try to persuade them: Ronn Blitzer, "FBI, DOJ Announce Indictment Against 8 Chinese Operatives," Fox News, Oct. 28, 2020, www.foxnews.com.

110 threatened over the telephone or online: Teng Biao, "No Escape: The Fearful Life of China's Exiled Dissidents," Al Jazeera, April 9, 2018, www.aljazeera.com.

111 the FBI arrested two people: "Two Arrested for Operating Illegal Overseas Police Station of the Chinese Government," Department of Justice, April 19, 2023, www.justice.gov.

111 The Dutch government says it has uncovered: Anna Holligan, "China Accused of Illegal Police Stations in the Netherlands," BBC, Oct. 26, 2022, www.bbc.com/news.

111 four men passing themselves off as Chilean police detectives: "Venezuelan Military Refugee in Chile Is Abducted from His Home in an Apparent Commando Operation," MercoPress, Feb. 22, 2024, en.mercopress.com; Catalina Batarce and Gianluca Parrini, "El inédito diario de torturas del teniente Ojeda," March 3, 2024, La Tercera, www.latercera.com.

111 conned into boarding a private plane: Ruth Maclean, "How a Savior of Rwanda, Paul Rusesabagina, Became Its Captive," *New York Times,* Sept. 20, 2021.

112 Indian agents are alleged to have murdered: Nadine Yousif and Neal Razzell, "Who Was Canadian Sikh Leader Hardeep Singh Nijjar?," BBC, Oct. 2, 2023, www.bbc.com/news.

113 Iran sends weapons and fighters: Will Fulton, Joseph Holliday, and Sam Wyer, "Iranian Strategy in Syria," Institute for the Study of War, 2013, accessed Feb. 20, 2024, www.understandingwar.org.

114 Russia's long-standing ties to Syria: Anna Borshchevskaya, "Russia's Strategic Success in Syria and the Future of Moscow's Middle East Policy," Lawfare, Jan. 23, 2022, www.lawfaremedia.org.

114 weapons built with Iranian assistance: James Ball, "Syria Has Expanded Chemical Weapons Supply with Iran's Help, Documents Show," *Washington Post,* July 27, 2012.

114 stopped sharing information with the UN: Kareem Shaheen, "MSF Stops Sharing Syria Hospital Locations After 'Deliberate' Attacks," *Guardian,* Feb. 18, 2016.

114 "Today in Syria, the abnormal": Don Melvin, "Syria Hospital Bombings Destroy Health Care, MSF Says," CNN, Feb. 18, 2016, www.cnn.com; Pamela Engel, "Russia Attacking Hospitals in Syria," *Business Insider,* Feb. 21, 2016, www.businessinsider.com.

115 "meticulously planned and ruthlessly carried out": Independent International Commission of Inquiry on the Syrian Arab Republic, "13th report of the Commission of Inquiry on the Syrian Arab Republic," Feb. 2, 2017, OHCHR, www.ohchr.org.

115 to claim that film or evidence of those attacks: "The Kremlin's Chemical Weapons Disinformation Campaigns," U.S. Department of State, May 1, 2022, www.state.gov.

116 a White Helmet volunteer testified: Scott Pelley, "What a Chemical Attack in Syria Looks Like," CBS News, Feb. 25, 2018, www.cbsnews.com.

116 I typed "White Helmets": Anne Applebaum, "Opinion: Russia Is Lying About Syria. But Trump Has No Credibility to Counter It," *Washington Post,* April 13, 2018.

117 "It is important to leave internal affairs": "Assad Gets Warm Recep-

tion as Syria Welcomed Back into Arab League," Al Jazeera, May 19, 2023, www.aljazeera.com.

117 "We decided to turn our mutual relations": Nike Ching, "Khamenei: Iran Never Trusted West, Seeks Closer Ties with China," Voice of America, Jan. 23, 2016, voanews.com.

118 These deals weakened the sanctions: Reuel M. Gerecht and Ray Takeyh, "The Mullahs and the Dragon," *National Review,* Dec. 21, 2023, www.nationalreview.com.

118 Wagner was funded and supplied: Jack Watling, Oleksandr V. Danylyuk, and Nick Reynolds, "The Threat from Russia's Unconventional Warfare Beyond Ukraine, 2022–24," Royal United Services Institute, Feb. 20, 2024, static.rusi.org.

119 the Iranian proxies share no ideology with Wagner: Bruce Riedel, "Hezbollah and the Axis of Resistance in 2024," Brookings Institution, Jan. 16, 2024, www.brookings.edu.

119 Hezbollah runs a political party: Nicholas Frakes, "How Hezbollah Uses Ramadan TV Shows to Bolster Its Image," New Arab, April 19, 2023, www.newarab.com.

119 Even before the coup: Kirsten Anna and Mohamed Keita, "Russia's Influence in Mali," Human Rights Foundation, Aug. 11, 2023, hrf.org.

120 They run a radio station: Auric J. Ouakara, Radio Lengo Songo, Feb. 13, 2024, lengosongo.cf.

120 a Russian diplomat instructed: Roger Cohen, "Putin Wants Fealty, and He's Found It in Africa," *New York Times,* Dec. 27, 2022.

120 In return for these services: "Wagner Group Uses Mafia-Style Tactics to Dominate CAR's Diamond Sector," *Africa Defense Forum,* Aug. 1, 2023, adf-magazine.com.

120 "regime survival package": Watling, Danylyuk, and Reynolds, "Threat from Russia's Unconventional Warfare Beyond Ukraine."

v *Smearing the Democrats*

122 "In recent years": Gene Sharp, *From Dictatorship to Democracy: A Conceptual Framework for Liberation* (Boston: The Albert Einstein Institution, 2002), 1.

124 Without Sharp's name: Ruaridh Arrow, "Gene Sharp: Author of the Nonviolent Revolution Rulebook," BBC, Feb. 21, 2011, www.bbc.com/news.

125 In a 1978 essay: Vaclav Havel, "The Power of the Powerless," Hannah Arendt Center for Politics and the Humanities, Bard University, Dec. 23, 2011, hac.bard.edu.

131 "They tell me that the green": Evan Mawarire, "#ThisFlag. The 1st Video That Started It All," video, YouTube, www.youtube.com.

132 Years later: Interview with Evan Mawarire, May 2023.

133 "pastor's fart": Jonathan Moyo (@ProfJNMoyo), Twitter, May 9, 2016, 1:41 a.m., twitter.com/ProfJNMoyo.

133 an alternative #OurFlag movement: Farai Mutsaka, "Zimbabwe's Flag Center of Social Media War over Frustrations," AP News, June 11, 2016, apnews.com.

133 Instead of merely trumpeting: From an interview with Evan Mawarire, May 23, 2023; also, "Supporters in Zimbabwe Fume After Protest Pastor Leaves for US," Voice of America, Aug. 21, 2016, www.voanews.com.

134 Cicero's brother Quintus: Philip Freeman, "Cicero, Dirty Tricks, and the American Way of Campaigning," *Wall Street Journal,* March 16, 2012.

134 "we intend to find the link": Bill Keller, "Innocent Googling? No Such Thing in Tehran," *New York Times,* June 16, 2009.

135 a reference to Soros: "Joint News Conference by Trump and Putin: Full Video and Transcript," *New York Times,* July 16, 2018.

135 Putin blamed Hillary: David M. Herszenhorn and Ellen Barry, "Putin Contends Clinton Incited Unrest over Vote," *New York Times*, Dec. 8, 2011.

135 "utilized by masterminds": Russian Ministry of Foreign Affairs, "'Euromaidan': 10 Years of Disappointment," Nov. 21, 2023, russianembassyza.mid.ru/en.

135 "Kremlin propaganda, the conviction": Timothy Snyder, "Ukraine's Maidan Revolution," *Thinking About . . . ,* Substack, Nov. 21, 2023, snyder.substack.com.

136 "another one of Pastor Mawarire's": "Mawarire Is No Saint," *The Herald,* July 23, 2016, www.herald.co.zw.

136 they are designed to make it impossible: Amy Slipowitz and Mina Loldj, "Visible and Invisible Bars," Freedom House, 2023, freedomhouse.org, accessed Feb. 16, 2024.

138 the Cuban government staged: David E. Hoffman, *Give Me Liberty:*

The True Story of Oswaldo Payá and His Daring Quest for a Free Cuba (New York: Simon & Schuster, 2022).

139 Chinese police beat Sun Lin: "Beaten to Death by State Security: RSF Shocked by Gruesome Murder of Independent Journalist in China," Reporters sans Frontières, Nov. 21, 2023, rsf.org.

139 Funerals in apartheid South Africa: Michael Parks, "South Africa Bans Public Protest at Funerals," *Los Angeles Times,* Aug. 1, 1985.

139 Funerals in Myanmar: "Funerals Become Scenes of Myanmar Resistance, More Violence," AP News, March 28, 2021, apnews.com.

140 So-called anti-extremism legislation: Mike Eckel, "'Extremism' as a Blunt Tool: Behind the Russian Law Being Used to Shut Navalny Up," RFE/RL, April 29, 2021, www.rferl.org.

140 Turkey, Eritrea, and Sudan: Marlies Glasius, Jelmer Schalk, and Meta De Lange, "Illiberal Norm Diffusion: How Do Governments Learn to Restrict Nongovernmental Organizations?," *International Studies Quarterly* 64, no. 2 (June 2020): 453–68.

140 An Ethiopian version: "Analysis of Ethiopia's Draft Civil Society Law," Human Rights Watch, Oct. 13, 2008, hrw.org.

140 Cambodia passed a law: Harriet Sherwood, "Human Rights Groups Face Global Crackdown 'Not Seen in a Generation,'" *Guardian,* Aug. 26, 2015.

141 In January 2024, Venezuela's National Assembly: "Venezuela: ONGs en Venezuela bajo grave riesgo," Amnesty International, Jan. 11, 2024, www.amnesty.org.

141 arrested hundreds of people: "Cuba: Freedom in the World 2023 Country Report," Freedom House, 2023, freedomhouse.org.

141 An illiberal Georgian government: Tina Dolbaia and Maria Snegovaya, "In Georgia, Civil Society Wins Against Russia-Style 'Foreign Agents' Bill," *CSIS,* March 15, 2023, www.csis.org.

141 Egypt has likewise: "Egypt: Crackdown on Human Rights Defenders Continues amid Ongoing 'Foreign Funding' Investigation," Amnesty International, July 30, 2021, www.amnesty.org.

141 Sudan used laws on security: Godfrey Musila, "The Spread of Anti-NGO Measures in Africa: Freedoms Under Threat," Freedom House, 2019, accessed Feb. 18, 2024, freedomhouse.org.

141 China passed a law: Tom Phillips and Christy Yao, "China Passes

Law Imposing Security Controls on Foreign NGOs," *Guardian,* April 28, 2016.

142 Henrique Capriles was also barred: Reuters, "Key Venezuela Opposition Figure Barred from Office for 15 Years," Voice of America, April 7, 2017, www.voanews.com.

143 the infamously corrupt Myanmar army leaders: Paw Htun, "Myanmar Military's Attempts to Smear Suu Kyi as Corrupt Have Failed," *Irrawaddy,* May 17, 2022, www.irrawaddy.com.

144 a system to transfer small amounts: Digital Forensic Research Lab, "#InfluenceForSale: Venezuela's Twitter Propaganda Mill," Medium, Feb. 3, 2019, medium.com.

144 "We all trust in Mohammed bin Salman": Brandtley Vickery, "Mohammed bin Salman's 'Army of Flies': Saudi Arabia's Creative Spread of Disinformation and Attack on Political Dissidence," Democratic Erosion, Nov. 30, 2021, www.democratic-erosion.com.

146 Certainly that was the case: Zosia Wanat, "Senior Polish Official Quits in the Wake of Internet Trolling Allegations," *Politico,* Aug. 20, 2019, www.politico.eu.

146 "Fuck off," she wrote: Magdalena Gałczyńska, "Troll Farm at the Ministry of Justice," Onet Investigation, Themis Stowarzyszenie Sędziów, Aug. 19, 2019, themis-sedziowie.eu.

146 The campaign against Denise Dresser: Interview with Denise Dresser, Feb. 2023.

148 bugged, harassed, and manipulated: Jonathan Eig, *King: A Life* (New York: Farrar, Straus and Giroux, 2023), 392–400.

148 President Richard Nixon sought: Michael E. Miller, "Nixon Had an Enemies List. Now So Does Trump," *Washington Post,* Aug. 19, 2018.

148 He published the telephone number: Mary Clare Jalonick, "Jan. 6 Takeaways: Trump's State Playbook; 'Hateful' Threats," AP News, June 21, 2022, apnews.com.

Epilogue: Democrats United

155 Cuban secret policemen: Dave Sherwood, "Special Report: How Cubans Were Recruited to Fight for Russia," Reuters, Oct. 3, 2023.

155 capture the disputed territory: Wendell Steavenson, "Nagorno-

Karabakh, the Republic That Disappeared Overnight," *1843 Magazine,* Jan. 1, 2024, www.economist.com.

155 Chinese hackers were discovered: 837 Parl. Deb. H.C. (6th ser.) (2024) col. 668.

155 a multinational investigation revealed: Pieter Haeck, "Russian Propaganda Network Paid MPs, Belgian PM Says," *Politico,* March 28, 2024.

157 "pose serious threats to global and regional peace": "Joint Statement of the Russian Federation and the People's Republic of China on the International Relations Entering a New Era and the Global Sustainable Development."

157 "sacred fight to punish the gathering of evil": "Full Text Transcript of Putin & Kim Jong-un Meeting," *Mirage News,* Sept. 13, 2023, www.miragenews.com.

157 "destroy the entity called the Republic of Korea": Johnny Harris, "Kim Jong Un Warns US Would Be Crushed in War with North Korea," YouTube, 2024, www.youtube.com.

157 "any version of Ukraine": "Dmitry Medvedev Says Ukraine Should Not Exist in Any Form, Calling It a 'Cancerous Growth,'" *Meduza,* Jan. 17, 2024, meduza.io.

157 a map of Russia: Andrew Osborn, "Putin Ally Says 'Ukraine Is Russia' and Historical Territory Needs to 'Come Home,'" Reuters, March 4, 2024.

161 seeking influence in the Biden administration: Josh Rogin, "Opinion: In May, Ukrainian Oligarch Said Giuliani Was Orchestrating a 'Clear Conspiracy Against Biden,'" *Washington Post,* Oct. 3, 2019; Ben Schreckinger, "Ukraine Scandal Ropes in Clinton-Era GOP Operatives," *Politico,* Oct. 3, 2019.

164 The GEC revealed the campaign: "The Kremlin's Efforts to Spread Deadly Disinformation in Africa," U.S. Department of State, Feb. 12, 2024, www.state.gov.

164 The German government revealed: Kate Connolly, "Germany Unearths Pro-Russia Disinformation Campaign on X," *Guardian,* Jan. 26, 2024.

169 cutting off Ukraine from gas supplies: Andrew E. Kramer, "Russia Cuts Off Gas to Ukraine in Cost Dispute," *New York Times,* Jan. 2, 2006.

169 and again in 2014: Jack Farchy et al., "Russia Cuts Off Gas Supplies to Ukraine," *Financial Times,* June 16, 2014, www.ft.com.

169 became enmeshed in German culture: Erika Solomon and Katrin Bennhold, "How a German State Helped Russia Complete Nord Stream 2," *New York Times,* Dec. 2, 2022.

169 an idealized version of Russian-German history: Judy Dempsey, "Exhibition Traces Ties Between Germany and Russia," *New York Times,* Dec. 20, 2012.

169 Schalke, a German soccer club: Tassilo Hummel et al., "The Meat Magnate Who Pushed Putin's Agenda in Germany," Reuters, May 31, 2023; "Designierter Bundespräsident Steinmeier liebt den FC Schalke," *DerWesten,* Nov. 15, 2016, www.derwesten.de.

169 Schröder was earning close to $1 million: Katrin Bennhold, "How the Ex-chancellor Gerhard Schröder Became Putin's Man in Germany," *New York Times,* April 23, 2022.

170 Chancellor Angela Merkel: Melissa Eddy, "German Government Nationalizes Gas Unit Seized from Gazprom," *New York Times,* Nov. 14, 2022.

170 In April 2023: "Remarks by National Security Advisor Jake Sullivan on Renewing American Economic Leadership at the Brookings Institution," White House, April 27, 2023, whitehouse.gov.

172 anonymous shell companies: Craig Unger, "Trump's Businesses Are Full of Dirty Russian Money. The Scandal Is That It's Legal," *Washington Post,* March 29, 2019.

172 also gave a speech: "Speech by President von der Leyen on EU-China Relations to the Mercator Institute for China Studies and the European Policy Centre," European Commission, March 27, 2023, ec.europa.eu.

Text Credits

Portions of this book originally appeared in the following publications:

The Atlantic: "Conservatives and the False Romance of Russia," December 12, 2019; "Venezuela Is the Eerie Endgame of Modern Politics," February 27, 2020; "A KGB Man to the End," September 2020; "How China Outsmarted the Trump Administration," November 2020; "How to Put Out Democracy's Dumpster Fire," April 2021; "Other Regimes Will Hijack Planes Too," May 24, 2021; "The Kleptocrats Next Door," December 8, 2021; "The Bad Guys Are Winning," December 2021; "America Needs a Better Plan to Fight Autocracy," March 15, 2022; "There Is No Liberal World Order," March 31, 2022; "China's War Against Taiwan Has Already Started," December 14, 2022; "There Are No Rules," October 9, 2023.

The Washington Post: "Let a Thousand Filters Bloom," July 20, 2005; "How the U.S. and Britain Help Kleptocracies Around the World—And How We Pay the Price as Well," May 13, 2016.

The Spectator (London): "Letting Russia into the G8 Gave Tacit Approval to Putin," March 3, 2014.

The New York Review of Books: "How He and His Cronies Stole Russia," December 18, 2014.

Index